TRAFFIC ACCIDENT
INVESTIGATORS'
MANUAL

ABOUT THE AUTHOR

R.W. Rivers is a graduate of Northwestern University Traffic Institute's traffic accident investigation and police management training programs. He has also completed training with the Canadian Institute of Science and Technology in technical mathematics and areas of physics, studied psychology at the Okanagan Regional College, studied police administration through the University of Minnesota, completed patrol management training with the IACP, developed the traffic accident investigation and traffic law enforcement training programs of the Royal Canadian Mounted Police and the course training standards for the Canadian Police College and University of Alberta in technical traffic accident investigation. During his 33 years service with the Royal Canadian Mounted Police, Inspector Rivers was employed extensively in general police work, highway patrol, accident investigation, research and planning, and training and development. Since his retirement, Inspector Rivers has acted as a consultant and has assisted in traffic accident investigation training on an international basis and accepted a position as adjunct faculty member and director of correspondence training with the Institute of Police Technology and Management (IPTM), University of North Florida.

Second Edition

TRAFFIC ACCIDENT INVESTIGATORS' MANUAL

A Levels 1 and 2 Reference, Training and Investigation Manual

By

R. W. RIVERS

Inspector, Traffic Branch
Royal Canadian Mounted Police (Retired)
Province of British Columbia
Canada

With a Foreword by

D. K. Wilson

Deputy Commissioner
Royal Canadian Mounted Police (Retired)

C H A R L E S C T H O M A S • P U B L I S H E R
Springfield • Illinois • U.S.A.

Published and Distributed Throughout the World by

CHARLES C THOMAS • PUBLISHER
2600 South First Street
Springfield, Illinois 62794-9265

© *1995 by* CHARLES C THOMAS • PUBLISHER

ISBN 0-398-05967-5 (cloth)
ISBN 0-398-05968-3 (paper)

Library of Congress Catalog Card Number: 94-40334

First Edition, 1981
Second Edition, 1995

With THOMAS BOOKS *careful attention is given to all details of manufacturing
and design. It is the Publisher's desire to present books that are satisfactory as to
their physical qualities and artistic possibilities and appropriate for their particular
use.* THOMAS BOOKS *will be true to those laws of quality that assure a good
name and good will.*

Printed in the United States of America
SC-R-3

Library of Congress Cataloging-in-Publication Data

Rivers, R. W. (Robert W.)
    Traffic accident investigator's manual : a levels 1 and 2
reference, training and investigation manual / by R. W. Rivers.—
2nd ed.
        p.   cm.
    1st ed. published under title: On-scene traffic accident
investigator's manual.
    Includes bibliographical references and index.
    ISBN 0-398-05967-5. — ISBN 0-398-05968-3 (pbk.)
    1. Traffic accident investigation—Handbooks, manuals, etc.
I. Title.
HV8079.55.R56   1995
363.2'5—dc20   94-40334
                                                              CIP

To Gertrude Sprenkle and in memory of Leo

FOREWORD

Webster defines an *accident* as a happening that is not expected, foreseen, or intended. He also states that in law, an *accident* is an unforeseen event that is not anyone's fault.

Many traffic "accidents" *are* someone's fault. Some are intended. Others can be foreseen. It is the traffic accident investigator's role to determine through the gathering of evidence and an analysis of circumstances, that which is an accident and that which is not. This Manual launches the trainee on the road to the scientific approach to determining which incident falls into what category.

Inspector Bob Rivers, Royal Canadian Mounted Police (retired), built his outstanding professional career around the theoretical and practical approaches to accident investigation and reconstruction. His expertise and reputation are recognized internationally. Few people would be as qualified as he to instruct the aspiring police person or the emerging traffic accident specialist on the correct scientific approach to traffic accident investigation.

Inspector Rivers' *Traffic Accident Investigators' Manual* will be an indispensable training guide and reference book for all who are required to bring the highest standards of professional endeavor to this complex facet of effective law enforcement.

D.K. Wilson

PREFACE

The traffic accident investigator must be aware of his or her responsibilities and how to properly fulfill them from the time of being advised of the occurrence of an accident to the time the report is completed based upon the investigation. Unless the investigator knows what type of evidence to look for and how to recognize, interpret, gather, and record evidence such as skid marks, yaw marks, roadway and vehicle marks and damages; and environmental, human and mechanical factors, improper conclusions may be arrived at regarding the accident cause. Of equal importance, the investigator must be aware of his or her limitations in an investigation and to know what evidence should be gathered and/or referred to those having particular expertise in specialized areas such as that found with the professional reconstructionist or with a forensic services facility. This manual is intended to meet all these requirements.

Mathematical equations and examples are completed in both the United States or Imperial and metric (SI) measurement systems. In many of the problem examples, exact conversions from United States to SI systems are not made or used in order to avoid an unnecessary use of multiple decimal places. Corresponding values in these cases should, therefore, be considered approximations. However, to assist the student or investigator, examples are worked out separately for each system and they should be considered independent of each other so as to avoid any unnecessary confusion.

Many published books and papers have been studied and tests conducted in the research and preparation of this manual. A bibliography lists several of these works.

The contents of this *Traffic Accident Investigators' Manual* are not intended to supercede policies or legislation that are now or may in the future be in effect in any jurisdiction. The views expressed herein are not necessarily those of the Royal Canadian Mounted Police.

R.W.R.

ACKNOWLEDGMENTS

The author wishes to acknowledge with thanks the permission granted by the Director, Institute of Police Technology and Management (IPTM), University of North Florida, to use IPTM training reference materials for inclusion in this manual. Most particularly from IPTM's *Speed Analysis for Traffic Accident Investigation Manual,* prepared by R.W. Rivers, in the areas of determining drag factors and speed analysis.

The author wishes also to acknowledge the *personal communication* (technical report) dated November 1, 1993, supplied by Dr. Bernard S. Abrams, O.D., specially prepared for the author and this manual. Dr. Abrams is the Director, Institute of Vehicular Safety, Columbus, Ohio, a researcher and lecturer specializing in the role of vision, visibility and discernibility in driver performance.

CONTENTS

TRAFFIC ACCIDENT INVESTIGATORS' MANUAL

Chapter 1

INTRODUCTION TO
TRAFFIC ACCIDENT INVESTIGATION

TRAFFIC ACCIDENT DEFINED

1.001   A *traffic accident* is *"that occurrence in a series of events which usually produces injury, death or property damage."* For the purposes of this manual, the term *traffic accident* is synonymous with the terms *accident, collision, crash* and *incident* or other similar, applicable term used in various jurisdictions and in many published works.

OBJECTIVES OF A TRAFFIC ACCIDENT INVESTIGATION

1.002   The objectives of a traffic accident investigation are to determine:
  a. **WHAT** happened, i.e., the type of accident.
  b. **WHERE** the accident occurred.
  c. **WHEN** the accident occurred.
  d. **WHY** the accident occurred, e.g., violation of law, engineering defects, etc.
  e. **WHO** was involved.

1.003   A traffic accident investigation can be divided into at least five segments:
  1. *Receiving the call.* As much information as possible should be obtained at this time, such as the precise location of the accident, any injuries sustained, and emergency equipment and other resources that might be required.
  2. *At-scene investigation.* This is perhaps the most important part of the whole traffic accident investigation process. In most cases, the success or failure of all other segments of the investigation depends almost entirely upon the evidence gathered during the at-scene investigation.
  3. *Follow-up investigation.* The at-scene investigation very often has its limits in terms of gathering evidence such as the taking of state-

3

ments of witnesses who do not remain at the scene, tracing the pre-scene paths and actions of those involved in the accident and the ability to conduct a thorough mechanical inspection of the vehicles involved. Under these circumstances, a follow-up investigation is required to gather or obtain this type of evidence.

4. *Reconstruction.* The reconstruction segment determines how the accident occurred based on all available evidence gathered at the scene or during the follow-up investigation.

5. *Accident cause analysis.* A cause analysis is carried out after the investigation and gathering of evidence is complete by taking into consideration and analyzing all aspects of the accident such as, but not limited to, the drivers, vehicles, roadway and other environmental factors.

AT-SCENE INVESTIGATORS' RESPONSIBILITIES

1.004   Upon the arrival at the scene of a traffic accident, the responsibilities of the investigator include:

   a. Caring for the injured.
   b. Protecting persons and property from further injury, damage or loss.
   c. Gathering evidence at the scene, including:
      (i) interviewing drivers, victims and other witnesses;
      (ii) examining for physical evidence, e.g., highway marks and damage and environmental factors; and
      (iii) conducting mechanical inspections of the vehicles involved.
   d. Recording facts including the taking of notes, statements, scene measurements and photographs.

1.005   Generally, an at-scene investigator should gather facts and information that will:

   a. Determine the cause of the accident.
   b. Provide information that will assist in accident prevention including *Engineering, Enforcement* and *Education* programs.
   c. Provide evidence for the prosecution in the event there has been a violation of law.
   d. Meet the requirements of accident report completion.
   e. Provide sufficient information to meet the requirements of follow-up investigation and reconstruction.

1.006 After completing the actual at-scene investigation, the investigator must ensure that all points of an investigation are completed by either personally carrying out any follow-up investigations that are required or by coordinating those investigations by others.

PERSONNEL SELECTION AND TRAINING

1.007 Any person assigned to traffic accident investigation, duties and responsibilities should:
a. Have a particular aptitude for traffic accident investigation.
b. Have a good basic knowledge of accident causes and investigational methods and techniques, and have at least a general knowledge of accident reconstruction principles.
c. Further his or her expertise and competency by taking training in advanced accident investigation techniques and undertaking self-study through various available literature and training courses.

INVESTIGATORS' INVENTORY

1.008 The investigator must have available equipment sufficient to meet the requirements of the various types of emergency situations and investigational requirements that might arise. An investigator should also be trained and totally familiar with the proper use of this equipment. All such equipment should be examined frequently and be well maintained. (See Table 1-1.)

Investigators' Inventory
Table 1-1

Axe	Single blade, head type
Blankets	Minimum of two, disposable type
Broom	Push type with heavy fiber bristles
Camera	Complete with necessary equipment, e.g., tripod, extra film, flash equipment, etc.
Carrying Cases	For camera and camera supplies, measuring tapes, traffic cuffs and vests, flares, fusees, etc.
Clinometer	For measuring grades
Clipboard	Portable type complete with light and plastic cover for rain
Coveralls	Suitable for conducting mechanical inspections on-scene
Crayons	Yellow color, lumberman's type, for marking positions of vehicles and other evidence
Dash Pad	For dash of vehicle, complete with light
Communications Systems	Radio communications system for vehicle and a public address system
Envelopes	For protecting evidence, e.g., paint chips.
Fire-extinguisher	Multi-purpose, dry chemical type
First-Aid Kit	Type and supplies dependent upon availability of other emergency services, e.g., ambulance
Flashlights	At least two, equipped with traffic wands
Forms	As required by departmental policies and legislation, e.g., statements and note-taking, field investigations, accident reports, inventory, etc.
Jack	Axle type for lifting vehicles in emergencies when bumper jack is not adequate
Knife	Sharp knife for cutting seat belts, clothing, etc.
Lights, vehicle	Emergency flashing lights; roof and side-mounted flood lights
Light, spot	Permanent mounted or portable pistol-grip spot light
Measuring Devices	a. Tapes
	b. Wheel
	c. Clinometer — for measuring grades and superelevations
Paper	Plain bond and graphic for preparing field sketches
Pencils	
Pry Bar	
Safety Vests	
Shovel	
Signs	Warning type signs
Tow Cable	
Tire Pressure Gauge	
Tire Tread-depth Gauge	
Traffic Cones	
Traffic (Arm) Cuffs	
Traffic Template	

Chapter 2

SERIES OF EVENTS

2.001 An investigator should be familiar with the various *events* that make up a traffic accident and ensure that the investigation covers all those events. For the purposes of traffic accident investigation, these various events are referred to as the *series of events*.

SERIES OF EVENTS DEFINED

2.002 For the purposes of traffic accident analysis, the *series of events* for a traffic accident includes *situations* that are in place or may at any time arise, all of which may be divided into two distinct categories:
1. *Pre-Scene Series of Events.* The events that lead up to the driver's point of possible perception of a hazard.
2. *On-Scene Series of Events.* The events that occur within the on-scene area, including the point of possible perception.

2.003 The pre-scene series of events can be further divided:
1. *Pre-trip Events.* Generally, those events that occur or that exist before the trip is started, including factors relative to the driver and vehicle, such as driver experience or inexperience, habits, impairment by alcohol or drugs, vehicle defects, or overload.
2. *Trip Events.* Generally, those events that occur or arise after the trip starts and lead up to the point of possible perception, including factors relative to the driver and vehicle, such as the driver stopping for a meal or a cup of coffee, driver fatigue, illness, consumption of an alcoholic beverage or a drug, erratic driving, view obstructions, vehicle mechanical failure or load falling from vehicle.

2.004 On-scene series of events include:
a. *Point of Possible Perception.* The place and time at which a normal person could perceive a hazard.
b. *Point of (Actual) Perception.* The point where a situation is comprehended or perceived as a hazard.

7

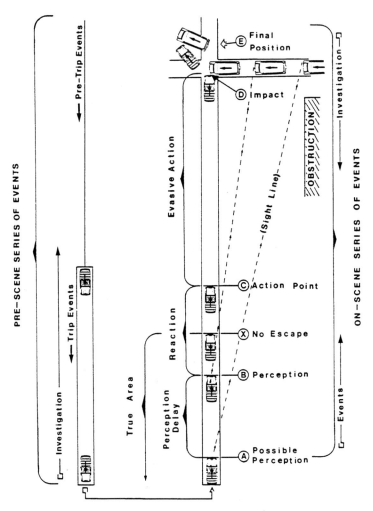

Figure 2-1. Series of events. Source: *Traffic Accident Investigators' Handbook* by Rivers. Courtesy Charles C Thomas, Publisher, Springfield, Illinois.

   c. *Perception Delay.* The time involved from the point of possible perception to the point of actual perception.
   d. *Perception Distance.* The distance traveled during perception delay.
   e. *Reaction.* The voluntary or involuntary response to a hazard or other situation that has been perceived.[1]
   f. *Reaction Time.* The length of time from when a person perceives a given situation as being a hazard to when he reacts to his perception. If a person's reaction time is unknown, 1.50 seconds

may be used for daytime investigation purposes and 2.50 seconds for nighttime.[2]

g. *Reaction Distance.* The distance traveled during reaction time.

h. *Action Point.* The place where a person takes action, such as braking or steering, based on his perception of a hazard. The action point follows reaction.

i. *Evasive Action.* The action or combination of actions taken (e.g., steering, braking) to avoid a collision or other hazardous situation.

j. *Evasive Action Distance.* The distance traveled from the action point to the place where a traffic unit stops or otherwise avoids a collision, or, if a collision is not avoided, to the point of impact.[3]

k. *True (Safe) Area.* The area leading up to the point of no escape in which evasive action could be initiated to avoid a collision.[4]

l. *Point of No Escape.* The place and time beyond or after which the accident cannot be prevented by a particular traffic unit.[5]

m. *Encroachment.* The entering or intruding into the rightful path or area of another traffic unit.

n. *Point of Impact.* The place, e.g., the point on the roadway, where a traffic unit strikes another traffic unit or some other object, or overturns.

o. *Primary Contact.* The first contact between two traffic units or a traffic unit and another object, or a vehicle's first contact with a highway surface during an overturn.

p. *Engagement.* The initial penetration of one traffic unit into another traffic unit or object during collision.

q. *Maximum Engagement.* The point or time at which there is maximum penetration by one traffic unit into another traffic unit or object during collision.

r. *Disengagement.* The separation of traffic units or a traffic unit and other object after maximum engagement.

s. *Secondary Contact.* A contact occurring when a traffic unit disengages from a primary contact and strikes the opposing traffic unit a second time or strikes another traffic unit or object.

t. *Post-secondary Contact.* A post-secondary contact occurs when a vehicle disengages from a secondary contact and again strikes the same unit or object or has a first or primary contact with a third traffic unit or other object. Under these circumstances, what may be a secondary contact for one unit may be the primary or first contact by another traffic unit.

u. *Final Position.* The location where a traffic unit comes to rest after collision. In determining the final position, it is important to learn whether the unit stopped at the position where it was found or whether it had rolled, been driven or moved to that position after the collision. For the purposes of this definition, final position does not include a position to which it may have been driven or forcibly moved, such as being towed by a tow vehicle, after it came to rest after disengagement.

v. *Personal Injury.* For investigation purposes, a personal injury is bodily harm caused to a person during the on-scene series of events.

w. *Fatal Injury.* A fatal injury is an injury that causes death during the on-scene series of events or a personal injury that thereafter results in the death of the injured person.

2.005 Each traffic unit (road vehicle or pedestrian[6]) involved in an accident has its own series of events. Each unit's series of events must be investigated separately.

2.006 Drivers and witnesses generally describe events forward, that is leading up to the result. An investigator, however, must start with the result and investigate back through the events as far as necessary to determine *where, when, how* and *why* the accident occurred.

CLASSIFICATION

2.007 Generally, the investigation of pre-impact collisions are classified as *visibility reconstruction* and post-impact are classified as *accident reconstruction.*[7] However, exclusive categories for classifying vehicle accidents, including those that result in personal injury or fatalities, should always be established or reported in accordance with state legislation and/or government or police department policies.

REFERENCES

1. Baker, J. Stannard: *Traffic Accident Investigation Manual.* Traffic Institute, Northwestern University, Evanston, Illinois, 1975, p.319.
2. Bernard S. Abrams, *Personal communication* (technical report) dated November 1, 1993.
3. Rivers, R.W.: *Traffic Accident Investigator's Handbook.* Charles C Thomas, Springfield, Illinois, 1980, p.25.

4. Rivers, R.W.: *Traffic Accident Investigator's Handbook.* Charles C Thomas, Springfield, Illinois, 1980, p.25.

5. Baker, J. Stannard: *Traffic Accident Investigation Manual.* Traffic Institute, Northwestern University, Evanston, Illinois, 1975, p.318.

6. National Safety Council: *Manual on Classification of Motor Vehicle Traffic Accidents,* 3rd ed. (ANSI D16.1). National Safety Council, Chicago, 1970.

7. Bernard S. Abrahams, *Personal communication* (technical report) dated November 1, 1993.

Chapter 3

INVESTIGATION PROCEDURES

PLANNING THE INVESTIGATION

3.001 During an investigation, the at-scene investigator must:
   a. Plan the steps he will follow so that his investigation will be conducted methodically and thoroughly from the time he received the report of an accident through to the time all persons, vehicles and debris have been removed from the scene.
   b. Guard against making unsound judgments by keeping an open mind and re-evaluating facts as he progresses through his investigation. He should place emphasis on gathering and recording facts rather than depending upon inferences and possibilities about how or why the accident occurred.
   c. Keep in mind that the "accident" may have been staged with an intent to defraud an insurance company or to cover up some other crime.
   d. Keep in mind that the "accident" may have in fact been a *suicide* or a *homicide*.

RECEIVING THE REPORT OF AN ACCIDENT

3.002 When the report of an accident is received, the investigator should be supplied with the following information, if possible, when he is dispatched to the scene:
   a. Precise location
   b. Severity, e.g., injuries to persons
   c. Disruption to traffic, e.g., blocked roadway
   d. Emergency equipment required, e.g., ambulance, fire-fighting equipment and/or tow-truck

PROCEEDING TO THE SCENE

3.003   When an investigator receives the report of an accident, he should proceed to the scene as quickly but as safely as possible. In deciding upon the urgency of the trip, the investigator should bear in mind the seriousness of the accident, particularly in terms of necessary aid for injured persons and the probable danger to other traffic.

3.004   The accident has already happened; therefore, although it is essential that there be no unnecessary delay in responding to the reported accident, high speed and driving in a manner that causes risk to other highway users should be avoided. An accident that has already occurred is not grounds to cause yet another accident. The investigator must not endanger his own life nor the lives and safety of others. He must use reasonable care and comply with local legislation respecting the use of emergency vehicles at all times.

3.005   While travelling to the scene, the investigator should:
   a. Select a route that will allow him to arrive at the scene safely and quickly.
   b. Watch for other vehicles and drivers that may have been involved in the accident or witnesses to the accident. Particular attention should be paid to vehicle damage, noting license numbers and descriptions of suspicious vehicles both while en-route to and upon arrival at the scene. This information may assist in locating witnesses or vehicles that were in some way involved in the accident.

ARRIVAL AT THE SCENE

3.006   Upon arrival at the scene, the investigator must carry out some duties immediately. The seriousness of the accident and assistance that is available will dictate how priorities must be established. Of immediate importance is protecting the scene from further damage or injury, and care for the injured. While this is being done, observations can be made of the scene to determine what evidence is available and ensure that sensitive or short-lived evidence is not removed, lost, destroyed or mutilated. Once the scene is secured in terms of protection and aid to the injured, an in-depth investigation may be conducted.

Protecting the Scene

3.007   An investigator should:
  a. Park his vehicle in such a manner as to be highly visible and to protect the scene. Emergency lights should be used as might be necessary. This is very important during darkness. Additionally, during darkness, park the police vehicle in such a way that the headlights will illuminate the accident scene. This will assist oncoming drivers in recognizing the situation and also assist the investigator in seeing the details of the accident.
  b. Not park his vehicle in such a way as to obstruct the safe movement of other vehicles and pedestrians that are free to proceed past the scene.
  c. Examine the scene for the possibility of fire, spilled or damaged hazardous cargo, e.g., chemicals, explosives, liquid fuels such as gasolines or radioactive materials. Where a danger exists, appropriate action—in terms of safeguarding the scene and notification to the appropriate authorities for advice and assistance—should be taken immediately. Procedures should be consistent with jurisdictional instructions, policies and procedures.
  d. Examine for downed or damaged electrical wires.
  e. Locate, collect or preserve short-lived evidence. If evidence at the scene, e.g., debris, vehicles, pedestrians, etc., must be moved before it is possible to measure and photograph its position, mark its precise location with chalk or in some other suitable manner so that proper measurements may be made later.
  f. Place sufficient warning devices, e.g., signs, reflectors, flares or fusees, and/or traffic cones on approaches to the scene to give adequate warning to other drivers and highway users. Use caution in lighting flares or fusees so that they do not cause fires or explosions when dangerous cargo or spilled gasoline is involved. Caution persons in the area not to strike matches or smoke when a danger exists.
  g. Not add to the confusion at the scene, endanger himself or others, or interfere with traffic by standing or walking in places that are not essential to carrying out a particular aspect of the investigation. For example, an investigator should not stand in a lane open to traffic to make notes, nor should he endanger the safety of a

witness or driver by having them stand in such places with him while a statement is taken.

h. Locate and identify drivers and witnesses. Take note of drivers and bystanders who could be potential witnesses at or near the scene. Obtain the names and addresses of as many witnesses as possible as well as the license plate numbers of vehicles parked at or near the scene. This information may be of considerable value during follow-up investigations.

i. Protect personal property and other items, e.g., vehicle parts, at the scene from theft or pilferage. Inventories of valuable items, particularly, should be made as soon as possible. When an item is released that is in possession of or under the control of the investigator, he should obtain a receipt.

j. Provide for the safe passage of vehicles and pedestrians and the resumption of normal traffic flow as quickly as possible. Whenever possible, a pointsman should be placed at a strategic location to facilitate the safe and orderly movement of traffic past the scene.

k. Request the assistance of regular police members when there is a heavy traffic volume, when the vehicles are situated in positions that obstruct or impede free traffic flow, and when the accident will result in a large number of onlookers and pedestrians. When crowds gather, it may be necessary to have assistance to remove intoxicated or disorderly persons, or others who interfere with the investigation. Assistance may also be required to remove impaired drivers.

l. Use civilians for traffic and crowd control only in emergencies. When it is found necessary to use civilians to direct traffic or to assist in crowd control, only those who appear to be responsible, competent and capable of carrying out the tasks involved should be selected. Civilians should not be asked to perform duties that are potentially dangerous. Volunteers should be given specific instructions respecting what is expected of them and how their tasks are to be performed.[1]

m. Block off the collision area in order to carry out a minute investigation for all possible forms of physical evidence, in some on-scene investigations, particularly hit-and-run accidents.

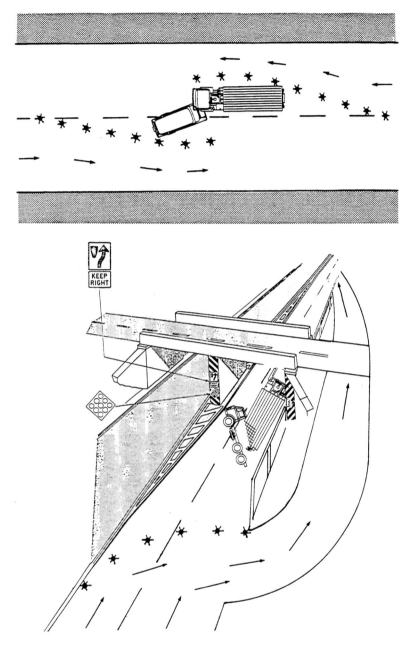

Figure 3-1. Methods of placing flares to assist in traffic control at accident sites.

Care for the Injured

3.008   One of an investigator's first and most important tasks upon his arrival at an accident scene is to ensure that injured persons are properly and adequately cared for. Depending upon the seriousness of the injuries sustained, the investigator should:

a. Determine as closely as possible the extent and nature of injuries suffered and examine the victim(s) for "Medic-Alert" tags or cards. Information gained should be given to medical and ambulance attendants, and hospitals.

b. Give or arrange for first-aid treatment.

c. Arrange for attendance of professional medical assistance and/or ambulance facilities. Seriously injured persons should be removed to proper medical facilities as quickly as possible.

d. Arrange for the coroner and other officials or persons, e.g., next-of-kin, to be notified of fatalities in accordance with legislation and departmental policy.

e. Mark the location of a victim on the highway before his removal and, if possible, photograph the location.

f. Ensure that all vehicle occupants and pedestrians involved in an accident are accounted for in case a victim was thrown from the scene area.

LEAVING THE SCENE

3.009   Before leaving the scene, the investigator must ensure that drivers are made aware of their responsibilities as drivers, injured persons and personal property are properly cared for, and the scene is left in a safe condition. The investigator should:

a. Advise the drivers which forms must be completed according to law.

b. Assist drivers in completing exchange of information forms.

c. Assist the driver by arranging for a tow vehicle or making other arrangements, when a vehicle cannot be removed from the scene by its driver.

d. Restore normal traffic flow.

e. Clear the scene of all debris and indications that an accident had occurred.

f. Ensure that each driver and others involved in the accident are safely on their way, offering any assistance that might be required.

REFERENCE

1. Rivers. R.W.: *Traffic Accident Investigator's Handbook.* Charles C Thomas, Springfield, Illinois, 1980, p.46.

Chapter 4

THE HUMAN ELEMENT

4.001 The ability of a person to control a vehicle on a highway must be a paramount consideration in any traffic accident investigation. The investigator should observe a driver or pedestrian for any sign of injury *not caused by the accident,* and for any other reason or condition that would lessen a person's ability to drive or walk safely, such as the following.

Injury

   a. Broken arm, hand or leg immobilized by a cast
   b. Impaired vision because of damage to eyes or swollen face
   c. Abrasions or bruises that cause slow, painful movement
   d. Amputations

Fatigue

   a. Signs of fatigue, sleepiness, drowsiness indicated by observations while talking to driver or pedestrian
   b. Driving long distances without stopping or resting
   c. Requirements of driving, e.g., driving a large, heavy vehicle for great distances, particularly when vehicle is not equipped with power steering
   d. Signs of "stay awake" pills in vehicle

Impairment by Alcohol or Drugs

   a. Odor of liquor on breath, and whether it is strong or weak and the kind, e.g., beer, etc.
   b. Muscular incoordination, including poor balance, staggering, weaving or swaying; slow, unsure reactions
   c. Unkempt appearance, clothes disarranged, dampness on trousers or clothing
   d. Difficulty in handling wallet, finding driver's license, dropping articles on roadway

19

e. Incoherent speech (thick or slurred), provocative attitude, using profanity, talkative and laughing, excited, crying (Note: a natural speech impediment might affect subject's speech).

f. Indications of legal or illegal drugs in vehicle, e.g., tranquilizers, barbituates, antibiotics, etc.

g. Indications of vomit in vehicle or on driver's clothing

h. Bloodshot eyes

Figure 4-1. Observations should be made for any indication that the driver had been consuming alcoholic beverages, e.g., beer, while in his vehicle.

Carbon Monoxide Poisoning

a. Carbon monoxide poisoning in a minor form may result in physical symptoms similar to alcohol impairment, e.g., headache, dizziness, weakness, impaired vision, impaired decision-making and impaired judgment. Advanced stages of carbon monoxide poisoning can lead to unconsciousness. When there are signs of possible carbon-monoxide poisoning, vehicle windows and air-vents should be checked to determine whether they are open or shut; the setting of air-conditioners should be checked, and the condition of the exhaust system should be examined.

General Health

a. *Vision.* Indications of impaired vision. Use or non-use of eyeglasses or corrective lenses.
b. Color blindness.
c. *Hearing.* Indications of hard of hearing. Use or non-use of hearing-aids.
d. *Illnesses.* Headache, common cold, etc.
e. *Disease.* Type and extent of any disease suffered by driver that could adversely affect his ability to drive safely, e.g., advanced stages of arthritis.
f. *Handicap.* Evidence of handicap that could adversely affect a driver's ability to drive safely. Drivers with some handicaps, e.g., partial loss of limbs, generally drive with more care and caution so as to compensate for their handicap. Some studies have shown that physically disabled drivers had a definitely lower accident rate than their non-disabled counterparts.[1]

Attitudes and Emotions

a. *Attitudes* and *emotions* are major factors in human behavior. A driver with a poor attitude towards his driving responsibilities, and a driver who is emotionally upset because of family or financial problems, for example, often result in driver behavior that causes traffic accidents.

Perception and Reaction

a. *Perception* is comprehending a situation, such as a hazard, by means of the senses and mind.[2] Reaction times of drivers in traffic are more correctly called perception-reaction times, because perception of a situation is usually involved.[3]
b. *Reaction* is defined as a person's voluntary or involuntary response to a hazard or other situation that has been perceived.[4] A driver should be observed for any indication of slow reactions to the extent that it could adversely affect his ability to respond to an emergent situation. There is a slowing of reaction time as individuals grow older, which begins to show between 35 and 45 years of age.[5]

c. *Reaction time* is the length of time from when a person perceives a given situation to when he reacts to his perception. The reaction time of a driver may properly be referred to as a *perception-reaction time.* When an individual's actual time is unknown, a reaction time of 1.5 seconds for daytime and 2.5 seconds for nighttime may be used for investigational purposes.[6]

d. *Simple reaction* is a response to an expected situation, such as responding to a traffic light. Approximately .75 minimum second is required for this response. *Simple reaction time* involving an uncomplex response such as touching the horn may be as low as 0.75 second. The reaction time required to apply the brake pedal after a situation is perceived is from 1.0 to 3.0 seconds for most people.[7]

NOTE: When there is range of time in seconds, it is recommended that calculations be made using the extreme time in seconds at either end of the range and at least one arbitrary time in seconds in the middle of the extremes. Such calculations will give the investigator a good idea of the upper and lower end of any calculation being made as well as a probably average of these.

e. *Perception delay* can occur because of such things as inattention or distraction. In many instances, actual perception immediately follows the point of possible perception and there is no perception delay. When perception delay is a factor, it is added to reaction time. When it is known that there is a perception delay but the precise length of time involved is unknown, 0.75 seconds may be used for investigation purposes.

f. *Reaction distance* may be calculated using Formula 4-1. [*See also* paragraph 2.004(g).]

Formula 4-1

United States	*Metric*
d = S × 1.466 × t	d = S × .278 × t

where d = distance
S = speed in mph (km/h)
t = time in seconds

The numbers 1.466 and .278 are constants used to convert speed in mph (km/h) to ft/s (m/s).

Example

A vehicle was travelling 50 mph (80 km/h). The driver had a reaction time of .75 second. He perceived a hazard and then reacted. The distance the vehicle travelled during the .75 second is calculated here:

United States	Metric
d = 50 × 1.466 × .75	d = 80 × .278 × .75
d = 54.97 ft	d = 16.68
d = 55 ft	d = 17 m

Pedestrians

The age of a pedestrian can be a contributing factor in vehicle-pedestrian accidents.

    a. *Elderly* pedestrians are particularly vulnerable to becoming struck by vehicles. This is often brought about because of impaired abilities to hear, see or otherwise perceive the danger of vehicular traffic. When a danger presents itself, an elderly pedestrian, because of lessened physical capabilities, is often unable to react quickly enough to avoid being struck. Many of these problems emanate from over-confidence regarding their own capabilities or those of a driver. For example, during darkness or at other times of limited visibility, it may be assumed by the pedestrian that because he is able to see the headlights of an oncoming vehicle, the driver can see him. Similarly, stepping out in front of an oncoming vehicle, feeling that the driver has sufficient time to stop, results in many accidents involving elderly pedestrians.

    b. *Children,* particularly the very young, are frequently the victims of traffic accidents. Because of excitement and general lack of attention, they may run into the path of a moving vehicle. This is often true in their local neighborhood where they have a false sense of security.[8] Young children, because of their generally small size, may not be seen by a driver as readily as a taller adult. As an example, a child playing in front of a parked car along the street would not likely be seen by a passing motorist until he darted out onto the roadway in front of the driver.

    c. A pedestrian's clothing color plays a large part in whether he is readily seen by a driver. During darkness, particularly if it is raining, dark colored clothing is extremely difficult to see in headlights unless it is reflectorized in some manner. During times of limited visibility, clothing colors may blend in with surroundings and the shade or color of the roadway.

    d. Pedestrians often carry flashlights to give warning to a driver. If there is a possibility that a pedestrian may have been carrying a flashlight but it cannot be found with the victim, examine the immediate surrounding area in the event it was thrown away by the force of impact.

4.002   Many details should be obtained from the pedestrian: What were the pedestrian's actions preceding the accident? Did the pedestrian look before stepping onto the roadway? Was his vision or hearing impaired? Was his full attention on what he was doing—such as on crossing the street? Was his mind on something else? When did he see the oncoming car? Did he think the driver would see him? Did he misjudge the car's speed? What is his attitude in regard to his personal responsibilities in traffic? Does he think it is entirely the responsibility of the driver to protect him? How well does he understand the problems and limitations of drivers?[9] (*See* Fig. 5-6)

4.003   The process of *smoking* may contribute to an accident in several ways. For example, a driver may lose control of a vehicle when he reaches into a pocket for a package of cigarettes, reaches for the cigarette lighter, drops burning ashes on his clothing or burns his fingers with a cigarette. The driver's clothes, particularly around the waist and upper thigh areas, and his fingers should be examined for burns which might indicate that he had been distracted for one of the reasons mentioned.

REFERENCES

1. Arthur D. Little, Inc.: *The State of the Art of Traffic Safety.* Automobile Manufacturers Association, Inc., June, 1966 (No address), p. 76.
2. Baker, J. Stannard: *Traffic Accident Investigation Manual.* Traffic Institute, Northwestern University, Evanston, Illinois, 1975, p. 318.
3. Evans, Henry K.: *Traffic Engineering Handbook.* Institute of Traffic Engineers, New Haven, Connecticut, 1950, p. 81.
4. Baker, J. Stannard: *Traffic Accident Investigation Manual.* Traffic Institute, Northwestern University, Evanston, Illinois, 1975, p. 319.
5. Evans, Henry K.: *Traffic Engineering Handbook.* Institute of Traffic Engineers, New Haven, Connecticut, 1950, p. 88.
6. Dr. Bernard S. Abrams, O.D., *Personal communication* (technical report) dated November 1, 1993, specially prepared for the author.

7. Dr. Bernard S. Abrams, O.D., *Personal communication* (technical report) dated November 1, 1993, specially prepared for the author.
8. Rivers, R.W.: *Traffic Accident Investigator's Handbook.* Charles C Thomas, Springfield, Illinois, 1980, pp. 54–55.
9. American Automobile Association: *Manual on Pedestrian Safety.* American Automobile Association, Washington, D.C., 1964.

Chapter 5

QUESTIONING DRIVERS AND WITNESSES

5.001   The drivers of vehicles involved in an accident and witnesses should be sought out and identified as soon as possible. Drivers may be seen writing down information from witnesses or from another driver, or be found standing near their damaged vehicles. Witnesses may be heard and seen describing to others how the accident happened. They may come forward and volunteer information or stand close by when the investigator is questioning drivers or other witnesses. They will often speak out, disagreeing with statements made by others.

5.002   Generally, in investigating accidents of a minor nature, witnesses and drivers may be interviewed and necessary statements taken at the scene.

Figure 5-1. During collision, a shoe or rubber may be forced from the driver or passenger. Its location may be later related to the seated position of its owner.

However, when the accident is of a more serious nature, particularly those involving serious personal injury or death, interviews and statements may have to be carried out later when a more formal and comprehensive interview can be conducted under more suitable surroundings and conditions.

5.003   The investigator should bear in mind that passengers and friends or relatives of a driver may give biased or slanted information. There are also witnesses who may wish to provide information to confirm their own interpretation of how the events of the accident occurred, which may not necessarily be factual.

DRIVER, PASSENGER AND WITNESS INFORMATION

Driver

a. Full name and address
b. Birth date
c. Telephone number
d. Driver's license number
e. Driver's license restrictions, if any
f. Compliance with driver's license restrictions, e.g., eyeglasses, hearing-aids, etc.
g. General health
h. Occupation

Passenger

a. Full name and address
b. Birthdate or apparent age
c. Telephone number
d. Occupation
e. Seated position

Witness

a. Full name and address
b. Birthdate or apparent age
c. Telephone number
d. Occupation
e. General health (particularly hearing and eyesight when these are factors)

Figure 5-2. A shoe found in a vehicle may assist in establishing the seating position of the person who was wearing it. The driver's identity may be established by matching imprints found on a shoe sole (*A*) with the tread patterns of the accelerator, clutch or brake pedal, (*B*).

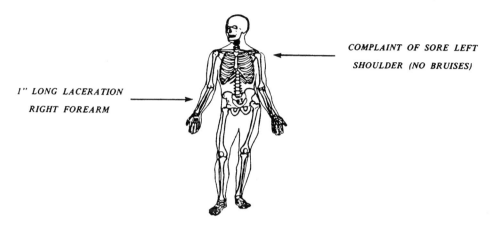

COMPLAINT OF SORE LEFT
SHOULDER (NO BRUISES)

1" LONG LACERATION
RIGHT FOREARM

Figure 5-3. An example of a diagram describing places and types of injuries sustained in a traffic accident.

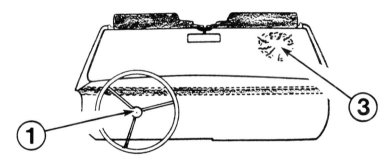

Figure 5-4. An example of a diagram showing occupant contact with interior of vehicle, which can be related to seating positions of driver and passengers as indicated in Figure 5-5.

Injuries

   a. Type and place of injury

INTERVIEWING DRIVERS AND WITNESSES

5.004   When interviewing drivers and witnesses, the investigator must be objective, be understanding and tactful, and exhibit a professional attitude and demeanor. He should:

   a. Ensure that an individual is in proper condition, both physically

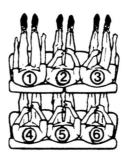

Figure 5-5. An example of a diagram showing occupant seating positions.

and mentally, to be interviewed, i.e., not suffering from serious physical injury, shock or emotionally disturbed to the extent that he may not comprehend what is expected of him.

b. Interview each driver separately, giving each of them an opportunity to express their own version of how the accident occurred without interruption.

c. Bring drivers together to compare their stories when drivers' views do not agree. Each driver should then be requested to repeat his version of how the accident occurred in the presence of the other driver so that conflicting areas may be clarified. When their stories agree and when the investigator is satisfied he knows how the accident occurred, he should bring the drivers together and relate to them his version of the accident events. He might also invite clarification on certain points at this time if he feels it is necessary.

d. Relate the drivers' versions of how the accident occurred to the physical evidence and other evidence that is available, e.g., damages to vehicles, inoperative or inadequate traffic control devices, witnesses' statements, etc. If the drivers' stories generally agree with this evidence, vehicles, other objects and obstructions may be marked for location and position and moved when it is essential that this be done or if it is necessary in order to restore normal and safe movement of traffic.

e. Have witnesses describe where they were and what they were doing at the time of the accident, e.g., driving behind one of the vehicles involved, standing alongside the roadway, looking out of a window, etc. At the same time, they should be asked what brought the incident to their attention, e.g., screams, squealing tires, noise from the collision, etc.

    f. The police warning or caution should be given to individuals being interviewed in compliance with the requirements of local legislation and policies.

5.005 Interviews should *support* an investigation. They should not be used to replace the need for an otherwise thorough investigation for facts and physical evidence. An investigator should make every effort to ensure that his interviews with drivers, pedestrians and other witnesses answer, clarify or corroborate information and evidence otherwise gained, or give leads for continuing or additional investigations.

QUESTIONING TO CLARIFY ISSUES

5.006 During an investigation, particularly during interviews of drivers and witnesses, there are many questions in the investigator's mind that can be answered or clarified. Some of these follow.

Distractions. Was the driver talking to a passenger in his vehicle prior to or at the time of the accident? If so, did what was being discussed upset or distract the driver?

Just before the accident occurred, was the driver looking at the roadway ahead, or was he looking to one side of the highway or the other? Did a billboard, pedestrian or something else distract his attention?

What was the noise level inside the driver compartment? Was it high enough that the driver may not have heard a siren, horn, etc.?

Was there an unavoidable distraction, e.g., did a wasp or other insect enter the vehicle? If so, how did it get in? Was a window or air-vent open?

Was the driver smoking just prior to the time of collision? Was he lighting a cigarette? Did he normally light a cigarette with a match or with the vehicle cigarette lighter? Did he drop his lighted cigarette? Were there indications of ashes or burns on his fingers or clothing?

Driving Abilities. Were the driver and vehicle compatible? For example, a small person might not be able to see over the dash of a large truck. A large truck without power steering may be difficult if not impossible for a small or weak person to control in an emergency situation. A large person might be seated too high in the vehicle to see overhead traffic signals.

PEDESTRIAN INTERVIEW REPORT

(Confidential Information)

Name _____	Address _____
(You need not fill in name and address if you do not care to do so)

Age _____	Sex _____	Nature of Injury _____
Do you have a driver's license? _____	Date you last drove a car _____
Were you feeling well at the time of accident? _____	Give date you were last sick _____
Do you own glasses? _____	Were you wearing them at the time of accident? _____
How long before accident did you drink an intoxicant? _____	How many years spent in school? _____
Were you with relatives or friends at time of accident? _____	Give number of friends _____
What color clothing were you wearing at the time? _____0. Dark _____1. Light _____2. Gray.
Did you see the car before it actually hit you? _____
How far away was the car when you first noticed it? _____ feet or _____ car lengths.

Physical Condition
_____0. Good health
_____1. Poor vision
_____2. Crippled
_____3. Poor hearing
_____4. Other defect: _____

Mental Condition
_____0. Normal
_____1. Trouble at home
_____2. Financial worries
_____3. Illness at home
_____4. Other trouble: _____

Attention
_____0. Normal—Watching traffic
_____1. Attention concentrated elsewhere
_____2. Was not watching traffic
_____3. Thought driver would stop
_____4. Other; describe _____

What were you doing at the moment you sensed danger?
_____ 0. Crossing at unsignalized intersection
_____ 1. Crossing with green signal
_____ 2. Crossing against red signal
_____ 3. Crossing intersection diagonally
_____ 4. Crossing between intersections
_____ 5. Walking on left side of roadway facing oncoming traffic
_____ 6. Walking on right side of roadway with traffic
_____ 7. Alighting from vehicle or trolley
_____ 8. In safety zone or loading zone
_____ 9. Playing in street
_____10. Other; describe: _____

What did you do when you first realized you might be hit?
_____0. Stood still
_____1. Ran forward
_____2. Jumped backward
_____3. Other; describe _____

How fast were you moving the moment BEFORE you sensed danger?
_____0. Standing still
_____1. Walking
_____2. Running
_____3. Other; describe _____

How far had you gotten across the street?
_____0. Just started across
_____1. Just ¼ across
_____2. About half way across
_____3. About ¾ across
_____4. Nearly across

How many steps had you taken from the last point of safety?
_____0. Steps from curb or walk
_____1. Steps from safety zone
_____2. Steps from trolley
_____3. Steps from bus
_____4. Steps from auto

What obstructed your view of approaching car?
_____0. Parked car
_____1. Moving car
_____2. Bus
_____3. Trolley
_____4. Pedestrian
_____5. Other; describe _____

Which way were you looking just BEFORE you sensed danger?
_____0. Straight ahead
_____1. To right
_____2. To left
_____3. Other; describe _____

What made you first notice the car approach?
_____0. Sound of horn
_____1. Noise from car
_____2. Warned by other pedestrian
_____3. Lights of car
_____4. Just happened to look that direction

Was this form filled out by pedestrian involved in accident? _____ If not, give name and relationship of
person making report.	_____

AMERICAN AUTOMOBILE ASSOCIATION
Traffic Engineering & Safety Dept.
Washington, D.C.

© ⒶⒶⒶ

Figure 5-6. Pedestrian Interview Report. (From the *AAA Manual on Pedestrian Safety.* Reproduced with permission of the American Automobile Association, Washington, D.C.)

Driving Education and Experience. What were the driver's driving education, experience and driving skills? How long had he been driving? Had he ever undertaken driver training courses? Did he have experience or training for the type of vehicle he was driving at the time of the accident? For example, had he developed any particular driving skills to drive a fully loaded, air-equipped transport truck if this happened to be the type of vehicle being driven at the time of the accident? How long had he been driving this particular type of vehicle?

Did the driver consider his actions leading up to the point of collision to be safe driving practices? If not, why not? What in the driver's opinion was the cause of the accident?

Evasive Action. What evasive action did the driver take to avoid the collision?

Illness or Injury. Did the driver suffer from an amputation or from a severe arthritic condition, stiff joints, rheumatism or other physical disability that might have affected his control over the vehicle?

What was the condition of the driver's eyesight and hearing. Was he color blind? Did his driver's license restrict him to driving with eyeglasses or a hearing-aid, outside rear-view mirror, etc. If so, was he complying with the restriction?

Did the driver suffer from a sudden illness, e.g., heart attack? If so, what was it?

Was the driver taking medication? When did he last take any form of medication? What was it? Was the medication prescribed by a physician? Was it taken in accordance with directions? Did the medication impair his ability to drive safely?

Did the driver suffer from a nervous disorder? Was he nervous, emotionally upset or aggravated because of some personal problem? Had he argued with someone shortly before the accident?

Did the driver bump his head or otherwise injure himself in the accident? Had evident injuries been incurred before the accident? Was his injury such that he could not adequately relate the circumstances surrounding the accident, e.g., pre-scene and on-scene events?

Impairment. Was the driver tired? How long had he been driving? How long was it since he last slept? How many hours sleep did he have? When did he last stop for a rest, have a meal or cup of coffee, etc.? Did he or could he have fallen asleep? Had he taken a form of medication to help him stay awake?

Was a window or air-vent open or partially open to allow fresh air into the driver compartment?

When was the last time the driver consumed an alcoholic beverage? What type of liquor was it? Had he been drinking by himself or with other persons? Who were they? At what time did he take his first drink? How much did he consume? Did he eat at the same time? What and how much did he eat? At what time did he finish his last drink?

Lights. Were the vehicle's lights on? Were the headlights on high or low beam? Were the headlights of an oncoming or a following vehicle on or off? If on, were they on high or low beam? Did the lights of other vehicles obstruct the driver's view causing him to become confused?

Was the driver proceeding in the direction of the sun? Could the sun's bright light have affected his view of the roadway or of other vehicles or thing collided with? What was the position of the sun visor?

Other Vehicles and Obstructions. Was there other traffic, vehicular or pedestrian, on the roadway just prior to the collision? Was other traffic following or meeting the driver?

How far away and what were the positions of other traffic when first seen?

Was there an obstruction on the roadway, e.g., rocks, roadway damage, construction, etc.? Did the driver see it? Could he have seen it? Did he try to avoid striking the obstruction?

Passengers. Did a passenger's seating position or actions in some way contribute to or cause the accident, e.g., talking, screaming, arguing, bumping or striking driver, obstructing driver's view, etc.?

Speed. Did the driver know what the legal speed limit was? Were speed signs posted? Where in relation to the accident were speed signs? Did the driver pass them? Did the driver know what speed he was travelling? When did he last look at his speedometer? If at night, was the speedometer face illuminated? In what speed graduations was the speedometer face marked? Did the driver feel that the roadway and weather conditions were such that the speed at which he was travelling was safe?

The Trip. What preparations did the driver make before commencing the trip? Where was he going to? Where had he come from? What was the reason or purpose in making the trip? Was the driver in a hurry, e.g., late for an appointment?

How familiar was the driver with the highway and the location where the accident occurred? How many trips had he made on this section of highway? When was the last time he travelled on this portion of highway?

Traffic-control Devices. Were traffic-control devices in place, e.g., traffic lights, directional markers, roadway markings, speed or stop signs, warning signs, etc.? If so, what were their locations? If they were a functional type, were they functioning properly? If they were signs or markings, were they properly placed, legible and easily seen? Did the driver comply with them?

Vehicle Action. Did the vehicle skid, slow down abruptly, spin, stop or go into yaw? Was the vehicle travelling forward, in reverse, turning or starting to move in one of these directions? Was the vehicle overweight, overwidth or improperly or unsafely loaded so as to make control difficult?

Vehicle Controls. Was the driver of sufficient size and strength to control the vehicle and operate its controls? Was he operating any of the vehicle's controls, e.g., gear shift lever, window crank, etc., just before or at the time of the accident?

What were the locations and condition of control mechanisms, e.g., brake, clutch, accelerator, dimmer switch, parking brake, gear shift lever (type of transmission), etc. Were the controls in a location that the driver may have accidentally touched one of them activating or setting the vehicle in motion?

Vehicle Mechanical Condition. Did the driver have knowledge of his vehicle having a mechanical defect? Did he feel that his vehicle might have been suffering a mechanical defect? What did he think the defect was? How did he feel it might have affected the safe operation of the vehicle? When did he intend to have the defect examined or repaired?

Were the windshield wipers in operation? Was the windshield being properly or adequately cleared? What was the position of the windshield wiper switch? If the windshield was not being cleared or cleaned adequately, why didn't the driver stop?

What was the position of the defroster or defogger switch? Were they in operation? Were they functioning properly?

When and where did the driver last service his vehicle? Who serviced it?

If the vehicle was equipped with a radio, was it on or off? Was the driver turning one of the radio controls? If the radio was on, what station was it tuned to? If on, what was the degree of volume? Was it loud enough that the horn or siren of another vehicle would not have been heard by the driver?

Vehicle Position on Highway. Did the driver know the place and position of his vehicle on the roadway just prior to and at the time of collision? At what point did he first realize there was a hazard? If the vehicle was in an unsafe or illegal position just before the point of collision, how and why did it come to be in that position?

Did the driver overtake and pass another vehicle just prior to the accident?

Visibility. Did the driver feel that he had good visibility of the highway, other traffic and surroundings leading up to and at the time of the collision? Was his view limited because of such things as his sitting position, dirty windshield or windows, stickers or decals on windshield or windows, passengers, load, glare from sunlight or artificial lights, etc.?

Weather and Road Conditions. What was the driver's impression of the weather conditions? Was the weather such that it limited his visibility, e.g., rain, fog, snow, etc. Was it daylight, dusk or dark?

What was the driver's impression of the roadway conditions? Were the roadway conditions such that driving was unsafe, e.g., slippery, potholes, rough, unpainted, too narrow, etc.?

Chapter 6

ENVIRONMENTAL FACTORS

HIGHWAY DEFINED

6.001   For the purposes of this manual, *highway* means *trafficway*.

Trafficway. A trafficway is any land way open to the public as a matter of right or custom for moving persons or property from one place to another.

Roadway. A roadway is that part of a trafficway designed, improved, and ordinarily used for motor vehicle travel or, where various classes of motor vehicle travel or motor vehicles are segregated, that part of a trafficway used by a particular class. Separate roadways may be provided for northbound and southbound traffic or for trucks and automobiles.

Exclusions: Bridle paths, bicycle paths.

Shoulder. A shoulder is that part of a trafficway contiguous with the roadway for emergency use, for the accommodation of stopped road vehicles, and for lateral support of the roadway structure.[1]

ENVIRONMENT

6.002   Make observations of the environment, i.e., the physical condition and make up of the highway, including adequacy of highway signs and traffic signals, road condition, engineering deficiencies, view obstructions, etc., the surrounding area for such things as billboards, and the weather conditions prevalent at the time. All or any one of these can be contributing factors in an accident. Make observations from a driver's or witness' line of sight. If the accident scene is not attended immediately, return to the scene on a following day, at the same time as the accident occurred and make the necessary observations.

HIGHWAY EXAMINATION

6.003   Examine the highway for:
   a. Roadway alignment with respect to the position of the sun, oncoming headlights, glare of sun off buildings or water, and ability to see traffic control devices or other traffic.
   b. Inadequate or improper roadway design, alignment of roadway center lines or lane markings at intersections; grade, width of pavement or shoulder, superelevation of curves, etc.
   c. Adequacy of advance warning signs or signals. Improperly placed signs or signals may not allow a driver time to take necessary caution or evasive action. Also, improperly placed speed reduction signs may cause a driver to slow down so rapidly as to contribute to rear-end collisions and chain reaction accidents.

Figure 6-1. The position of the sun can obscure a driver's view of traffic-control devices such as traffic lights.

   d. Maintenance of traffic control devices such as obliterated wording, non-functioning signals, etc.
   e. Positioning of traffic control devices, e.g., positioned in such a manner that they cannot be readily seen or in such a way as to

divert a driver's attention from his direction of travel and other traffic.

  f. Highway information signs or other signs, vegetation, parked vehicles, etc., in locations that obstruct the clear view of traffic control devices.

  g. Roadway surface markings, e.g., shoulder and lane markings, center lines and stop lines, particularly their locations, visibility, maintenance and adequacy.

  h. Position, height and distance from roadway of traffic control devices.

  i. View obstructions:

    1. General view obstructions, e.g., billboards, signs, hedges, parked vehicles, fences, shrubbery or other vegetation, trees, embankments, snowbanks, etc. These are particularly important in intersection accidents.

    2. Position, height and distance from roadway of any obstruction.

    3. Distance on approach that obstruction could be seen and whether and where it could be perceived as an obstruction.

  j. Shadows cast by buildings, trees, billboards, etc., that might obscure a driver's view of a pedestrian or other object.

  k. Highway defects or obstructions that might cause a vehicle to go out of control, e.g., soft shoulders, shoulder lip or drop-off, pot holes, ruts, etc.

  l. Inadequate street lighting. This is particularly important in pedestrian accidents.

  m. Glare from fixed lights, e.g., overhead flood lamps at used car lots or parking lots, and lamps used to illuminate buildings for security purposes.

  n. Roadway conditions, e.g., wet, dry, mud, snow or ice; and, slippery roadway surfaces caused by inclement weather, spilled oil, warm tar or asphalt, wet wooden bridge base, or moisture on dusty or dirt road surfaces.

WEATHER CONDITIONS

6.004 Check at the scene for weather or atmospheric conditions that might have been a contributing factor in an accident. Adverse weather conditions affect visibility, and also affect the handling capabilities of vehicles because of the effect on the coefficient of friction of the roadway.

Figure 6-2. Shrubbery, improperly placed traffic-control devices, buildings and parked vehicles can obstruct a driver's view of approaching traffic at an intersection and his ability to enter an intersection safely.

6.005 *Smoke* and *fog* will often be found in patches. Fog patches will most often be found in low lying areas. Smoke may be found in both high and low areas. The effects in terms of visibility are identical. The driver upon entering smoke or fog patches often decelerates abruptly. A following vehicle may strike the rear-end of the preceding vehicle. Such collisions may further cause sideswiping or head-on collisions with traffic approaching from the opposite direction.

Figure 6-3. The roadway should be examined for any defect or obstruction that could cause a vehicle to go out of control, such as in *A* and *B*. If the wheel of a vehicle drops over a lip as in *B*, the driver may not be able to steer it back onto the roadway, or if he oversteers, the vehicle may veer across the highway out of control.

ENVIRONMENT   OBSERVATIONS AND COMMENTS

Business
  Industrial
  Shopping
Playground
  General
  School
Residential
  Apartment
  Family
Recreational
  Park
  Camping
Rural
  Agricultural
  Other

Highway

Number of lanes
Lane markings
Bridge
Tunnel
Other, e.g., parking lot
Exit or entrance ramps
Intersection
Speed zone

Roadway Characteristics

Horizontal
  Curve
  Straight
Vertical
  Flat
  Hillcrest
  Hollow
Under construction
Defects
Markings
Maintenance
Surface
  Asphalt
  Brick
  Concrete

Figure 6-4. Environmental investigation guide.

ENVIRONMENT   OBSERVATIONS AND COMMENTS

Roadway Characteristics (Continued)

    Earth
    Gravel
    Oiled
    Stone
    Dry
    Wet
    Muddy
    Snow
    Ice
    Slush

Traffic-Control Devices

Type (Specify)
Obstructed
Obliterated

Light and Weather Conditions

Light
    Daylight
    Darkness
    Dawn
    Dusk
Weather
    Fog
    Hail
    Sleet
    Mist
    Snow
    Rain
    Cloudy
    Crosswinds

Visibility Obstructions

Hedges
Foilage
Trees
Building
Sign
Hill
Curve

Figure 6-4 continued.

REFERENCE

1. National Safety Council: *Manual on Classification of Motor Vehicle Traffic Accidents,* 3rd ed. (ANSI D16.1). National Safety Council, Chicago, 1970.

Chapter 7

HIGHWAY AND VEHICLE
MARKS AND DAMAGES

7.001 Evidence of marks, damage and debris suffered by or found on vehicles and highways will, if intelligently gathered and interpreted, assist in determining, and in some cases conclusively establish, a vehicle's (or pedestrian's) direction of travel, placement and position and behavior during times of pre-collision, collision and post-collision. It is essential, therefore, that an on-scene investigator knows what evidence to look for and be able to recognize and interpret this evidence.

HIGHWAY DAMAGE

7.002 *Roadway* damage includes:
   a. *Chip* or *Gouge.* A concave, chiplike cavity in a roadway surface.

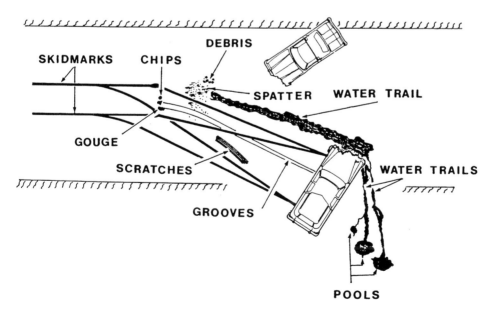

Figure 7-1.

45

Figure 7-2. *Chips* and *gouges* at *A* and a *groove* at *B*.

b. *Groove.* A channel or rut caused by a metal protrusion such as a bolt.

c. *Hole.* A cavity in a roadway surface that is round with smooth walls and is usually caused by protruding bolts, broken rods or similar round body objects.[1]

d. *Scrape.* A wide, superficial wound, or a wide, clean graze mark caused by a sharp or angular metal edge being passed over the highway surface, e.g., vehicle part sliding over roadway.[2]

e. *Scratch.* A long, narrow superficial wound.

f. *Striations.* Narrow, light, parallel stripes or streaks usually made by friction or abrasion on the *roadway* or on *vehicle* parts.[3]

7.003 A vehicle part may drop down onto the pavement causing a *gouge* and then as it proceeds, the part may rise and damage the surface in the form of a *scratch, groove* or *scrape.* Similarly, a vehicle part may begin by scratching the surface but as the weight becomes greater it may dig into the surface, e.g., pavement, causing a *gouge, chip* or *groove.*

Figure 7-3. A groove, *A,* can show a vehicle's direction of travel and whether it traveled straight or rotated after collision. Note slight rotation at *B.*

7.004 It is very important to remember that it takes two things to cause damages and marks, e.g., a vehicle and a highway surface. This is particularly important because when these damages or marks are caused,

Figure 7-4. During braking, the rear end of a vehicle rises, *A,* and the front end dips, *B.* When there is a rear end impact, the front tires of the following vehicle will often leave a *scrub mark* at *C.* This mark will help in establishing the point of impact. If the impact and downward thrust is great enough, the front end of the following vehicle, *number 2,* may be forced onto the roadway surface resulting in contact between underparts and the roadway. The damages suffered by the roadway may be in the form of chips and gouges and possible scratches or grooves, at *D.* These damages can be matched to the vehicle part that caused them thereby determining the placement of vehicles on the roadway at the time of impact. In rear-end collisions, after vehicles are disengaged, damages may not appear to match up because of vehicle action during braking. (*See* Fig. 7-5.)

the things that caused them had to be in certain positions and locations and their positions and locations had to have certain relationships to each other. For example, when two vehicles collide head-on, their rear-ends lift and the front-ends are forced downward. During this downward thrust, the front tires will often leave scrubmarks and underside and broken parts, such as tie-rod ends, will often dig into the highway surface causing unique damage and marks. By relating the highway surface marks and damage to the vehicle parts that caused them, it is possible to determine the vehicle's location and position at the time the marks and damage were caused.

7.005	Caution must be exercised in identifying roadway marks. Marks may be caused or left by passing vehicles before and immediately after

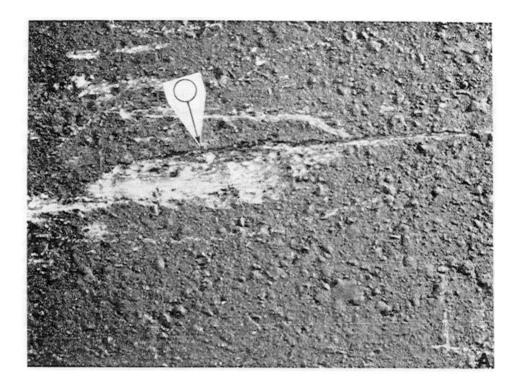

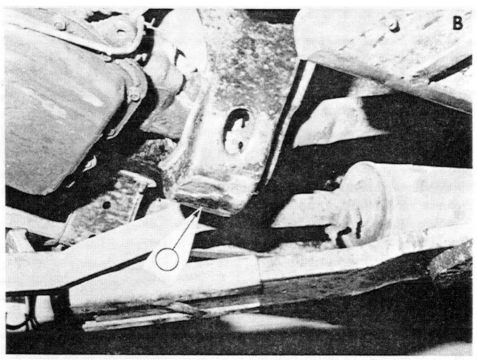

Figure 7-5. When vehicles collide, their underparts will often come into contact with the roadway surface. Damages occur to both the roadway surface (A) and a vehicle part such as a crossmember, tie rod end, etc. (B). By matching these damages, a vehicle's position on the roadway at the time of collision can be determined. (*See also* Fig. 7-4.)

Figure 7-6. Incidental damage at *A* (buckled roof and windshield damage) caused as an indirect result of a side collision and impact damage at *B*.

an accident. These may show up in photographs but do not, in fact, have any significance in connection with the accident under investigation.

VEHICLE DAMAGE

7.006   The damage suffered by a vehicle will assist in determining *how* and *why* an accident occurred. For matching purposes, the investigator should look for such vehicle damages and marks as:
  a. Dents and structural damage
  b. Paint scrapings or rub-offs
  c. Abrasions
  d. Scratches
  e. Striation marks
  f. Tire imprints

7.007   Damages are important for various purposes including position and angle at time of initial contact, direction of travel and speed estimates and, therefore, must be properly assessed and accurately recorded.

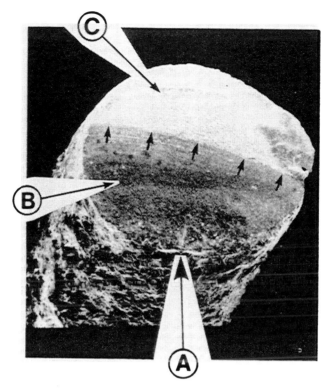

Figure 7-7. Fracture surface of a metal break. *A* denotes fatigue origin area; *B* and the arrows indicate the extent of fatigue cracking from the origin, and *C* denotes new and completed fracture. Note the discoloration of old cracking at *B* and clean, shiny, gritty area of recent fracture at *C*. (Courtesy National Transportation Safety Board, Washington, D.C.)

Care must be taken, however, to establish and differentiate pre- and post-collision damage. For example, a vehicle might have been damaged in a recent, previous accident or it might have suffered some damage in its removal by a tow-truck.

7.008 *Incidental damage* is damage that is incidental to engagement elsewhere on a vehicle, e.g., trunk lid forced open, roof buckling, window breakage, etc.[4] It is very important to distinquish between *direct contact damage* and incidental damage because to conclude that incidental damage was contact damage could very well lead to improper vehicle positioning at time of collision.

7.009 Immediately after an accident, a scraped or damaged metal part will be bright in appearance. Later, however, as with most metal materials, this brightness will diminish or disappear as it begins to rust. A previously

Figure 7-8. A vehicle's path of travel and movement may be traced from scratches, damages and marks left on highway fixtures and roadway by matching vehicle damages to these damages and marks. Such damage or evidence as at *A* will often answer the question as to why a vehicle reacted as it did, e.g., veering into opposing lane after striking an abutment.

broken or damaged part will most often be rusty in appearance. A recent break will be clean and shiny. A part that had a previous partial break and becomes totally broken will have both a rusty section and an adjoining shiny section on the face of the break. When there is an indication of a paint rub-off or scrapings from another vehicle or object in a damaged vehicle area, it should be closely examined to determine whether it might be undercoating or another layer of paint on the vehicle itself.

MATCHING DAMAGES

7.010 By matching or relating damages suffered by a vehicle and the thing struck, including the roadway surface, a vehicle's direction of travel, placement on the highway, point of collision and path followed both before and after collision may be determined.

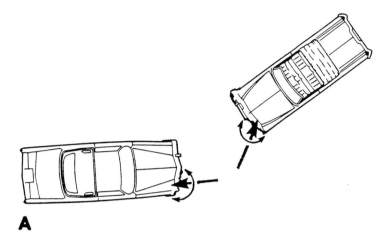

A

Figure 7-9A An example of a post-collision situation (*A*) where positions of vehicles at the time of initial or primary contact must be established. Directions of thrust (force between things coming into contact) and contact damage areas are indicated by arrows. Directions of thrust must be in line with each other, as in *B*. To place both vehicles in their positions at time of initial contact may be done diagrammatically by preparing a diagram of each vehicle to scale showing all individualisms or characteristics of damaged parts and directions of thrust. Use tracing paper (or heavy paper cut out to indicate damages), bringing both diagrams together, and maneuvering them into position until opposing damages match up as in *B* (*See also* Figs. 7-10 and 7-11).

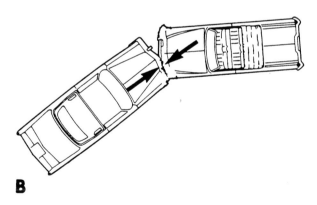

B

Figure 7-9B.

7.011   Roadside objects, e.g., sign posts, parked vehicles, guard rails, bridge parts, etc., may be gouged, bent, scratched, have paint scrapings or other indications of damage caused by a vehicle. By relating these

Figure 7-10. The angle of collision should be measured, photographed and recorded. Overhead photographs should be taken and overhead diagrams should be made. This information is useful in determining vehicle placement on the highway and direction of travel just prior to and at the time of collision (*See also* Fig. 7-9.)

types of damages to damage suffered by a vehicle, the vehicle's initial direction of travel and its path at the time of collision and post-collision can often be established.

7.012   During maximum engagement, a vehicle will maneuver and often rotate before disengagement. These movements leave identifying scratches and grooves. A close examination of these marks will assist in establishing the angle of collision and direction of *thrust* (the *force* applied against a traffic unit which is concentrated on a particular point on that unit at any instant during a collision) at the time of initial or primary contact, and the direction of rotation up to and until the time of engagement.

7.013   After colliding, a vehicle's underparts may leave scrapes, scratches and grooves as it leaves the collision point—from which the vehicle's path may be traced. If these marks are straight, it would indicate that the vehicle traveled in a straight line; however, if they are curved, it would

Figure 7-11. By bringing vehicles together, damages and points of comparison may be identified and related. Photographs and measurements should also be taken.

indicate that the vehicle was rotating or spinning after collision. (*See* Fig. 7-3).

7.014   Roadway evidence may be lost, damaged or destroyed by passing vehicles or pedestrians, rain, wind, etc. In situations where the on-scene investigator feels it is necessary to have someone else examine skid marks, tire prints or other roadway evidence, or when there may be a delay in making a proper and thorough examination, the area should be blocked off or otherwise protected to preserve the evidence.

7.015   A diagram or sketch should be prepared showing the place and appearance of a vehicle's damaged areas together with adequate measurements. Photographs should be taken from various angles. Both sketches and photographs of vehicle damages should be made from an overhead view. These are particularly important for matching up damages between vehicles and between vehicles and other objects, either photographically or diagrammatically or by a combination of both.

7.016   Precise measurements of and between undercarriage parts that caused highway surface damages should be taken. Similarly, measurements of highway surface marks should be taken so that they can in turn be matched to vehicle parts. In this way, the vehicle's position on the highway at the time the surface marks were made can be determined. When striation marks appear on vehicle parts and/or highway surfaces, measurements should be taken at right angles to the marks for matching purposes.

7.017   One of the best times to check the vehicle's undercarriage is when it is lifted by a tow truck for a tow-away operation. An examination

Figure 7-12. Measurements should be taken of scratches, *A* and *B*, as well as the vehicle parts that caused them, for matching purposes. Note the beginning of the skid marks, *C*, commences at approximately the same point as the scratches. Both scratches and skid marks help to establish a vehicle's position on a roadway at the time of collision and its subsequent path.

Figure 7-13. When a vehicle skids or sideslips on a turfed or soft surfaced area, grass or other material may become lodged between the tire bead and wheel rim. The direction of wheel movement is toward the side on which the material is embedded.

can also be made by raising the vehicle with a jack or on a garage hoist. When a vehicle is lifted, an examination should be made for parts that are scraped, scratched, bent or otherwise damaged, and which have highway surface materials embedded in them, e.g., grass, asphalt, gravel, etc. If the highway surface was soft at the place of contact, the undercarriage may have only a slight indication of abrasion, if any, but may have considerable surface material attached to it. (*See* Fig. 7-5B.)

7.018 Grass, sand and gravel may be found lodged between a tire and rim on the lead side after a wheel has undergone a sideways thrust with considerable force. This occurs when the tire is pushed away from the rim, allowing foreign materials to become embedded between the tire bead and rim. When the force diminishes, the tire returns to its original position, pinching the material between the tire and rim. If the force is too great, the tire may be forced off the rim.

7.019 When a vehicle strikes a pedestrian, the place and type of injury suffered should be matched to the vehicle part that caused it. Indications

Figure 7-14. In pedestrian accidents, a vehicle should be inspected for indications such as clothing imprints, handprints or damage that might be related or matched to contact with the pedestrian.

Figure 7-15. Sometimes the approximate point of impact with a pedestrian may be determined by the locations where things being carried by the pedestrian or articles of clothing strike or are left on the ground. Consideration must be given to the fact, however, that these articles might have been carried or thrown to the points where they are found.

of pedestrian contact to look for on a vehicle are blood, clothing imprint or fragments, hand prints, flesh, dents, etc. If the pedestrian is run over, look for similar evidence on the vehicle's undercarriage. Such evidence is useful in establishing the pedestrian's location at the time of primary contact.

7.020   When a vehicle brakes and there is rapid deceleration, the front end dips because of a weight shift to the front. Under these circumstances, the front-end damage of a following vehicle will often appear to be too high to match up to the rear-end damage of a preceding vehicle. This should be borne in mind when investigating rear-end collisions where a following vehicle brakes and slides into the rear-end of another vehicle (*See* Fig. 7-4).

TIRE MARKS

7.021   *Tire marks* are left on a highway surface by one or a combination of rotating, sideslipping, sliding or skidding tires. Considerable information can be obtained from these marks in terms of a vehicle's placement on a highway and its behavior at times of pre-collision, point of primary contact and post-collision. Of utmost importance of course, is to identify the tire that caused each individual mark.

7.022   A rotating tire travelling in soft material, e.g., mud or snow, will cause a sunken tire track or *rut*. The additional feature of a rut is that a tire imprint will be found at the bottom of the rut. A skidding or sideslipping tire and wheel or other vehicle part in soft surface materials will result in a trench or *furrow*. Ruts and furrows are useful in determining the path and direction a vehicle followed. They are frequently the extension of a skid or yaw mark as a vehicle leaves a roadway and travels across a soft shoulder or onto snow, mud or other soft material off the highway.

7.023   An *acceleration mark* is caused by a spinning drive wheel on a highway surface. The beginning of the mark on a paved surface will show a "burn" mark if the acceleration is great. As the vehicle begins to gain momentum, the mark will show two dark, outside parallel lines and parallel tire tread rib markings. As the vehicle gains speed, only the outside lines will show and they then disappear when the wheel is no longer spinning. Caution must be taken not to confuse acceleration marks with front tire skid marks, which have a similar appearance.

Figure 7-16. *Ruts* caused by rotating wheels in soft material (dirt) at *A*. Note tire prints leading up to the point where ruts begin. The vehicle's brakes were applied at *B*, pushing the material ahead of the wheels to cause a *furrow*.

Figure 7-18A. Acceleration marks show dark outside parallel lines at *A*, caused by *cupping* of tire because of downward thrust of weight, and parallel tread marks at *B*. If acceleration is great, burn marks or pavement melting may show as at *C*. *A* is an example of *reverse-forward acceleration marks*.

Figure 7-18B. A *studded tire* will leave striation or scratch marks when a wheel spins under acceleration.

Figure 7-18C. A tire will suffer striation or scratch marks when it spins on a gravel or gritty surface. If a spin is on a smooth surface, the tread will have a cleaned appearance.

Figure 7-19. Tire print caused by a rotating tire. A tire print will show the tread pattern, *A*. The numbe rof dark lines, *B*, indicate the number of tire tread ribs. Tire tread ribs will often leave similar dark lines in a straight skid but without the tread pattern. (Source: *Traffic Accident Investigators' Handbook* by Rivers. Courtesy Charles C Thomas, Publisher, Springfield, Illinois.)

Figure 7-20. When an accident occurs, fluids are often released onto the roadway. Crossover tire prints, *A* and *B*, must not be confused with tire or skid marks that are directly related to the accident.

7.024 A *tire print* is a tire tread impression of a rotating tire. A tire print may be left by a wet tire tread when it rolls on a hard, smooth surface; or, when it rolls in a soft or soft and wet surface such as when it makes a rut. Tire prints can be distinguished from skid marks by crosswise patterns of a tire tread. A straight skid mark may leave parallel lengthwise grooves showing the groove pattern of the tire tread, but there will be no crosswise pattern markings.

tires. Under these various circumstances, the tires will most often leave dark parallel lines at the outer edges of the tire tread. (*See also* Fig. 7-24.)

7.025 Use caution in relating tire prints to vehicles involved in an accident. Passing vehicles may drive through liquid debris at the scene and consequently leave tire prints as they proceed.

7.026 A *properly inflated tire* provides complete tire tread contact with the roadway surface under normal driving situations. Overinflated, undcrinflated and overloaded tires have unique configurations in terms of their contact with the roadway surface, resulting in unique tire and

Figure 7-21. *Underinflated tire mark.* Note the somewhat uneven edge lines. (*See also* Fig. 7-24.)

Figure 7-22. Overloaded tire mark caused by an overloaded single wheel. (*See also* Figs. 7-21 and 7-23.)

Figure 7-23. *Overloaded* or *underinflated* tire mark caused by a weight shift to the side of the tire as it travels around a curve. These marks should not be confused with yaw marks.

Figure 7-24. Flat tire marks: When a tire is deflated, it "flops" as it rolls. (*See also* Fig. 7-21.)

Figure 7-25. Bounce skid mark: Wheel is raised at *A* giving tire the shape of an overinflated tire with only the center portion touching roadway. Full weight on tire at *B* causing full tread contact.

skid marks that, if understood and properly interpreted, assist in accident investigation (*See* Figs. 8-15 and 8-19).

7.027 An *underinflated tire* (or overloaded tire) causes the tire tread face to "cup" and consequently the greater part of the vehicle's weight is carried on the tire's outer edges. A similar action occurs to the front tires when there is a weight shift to the front caused by severe braking action. Also, under extreme acceleration, there is a weight shift onto the rear tires. Under these various circumstances, the tires will most often leave dark parallel lines at the outer edges of the tire tread. (*See also* Fig. 7-24.)

7.028 A *deflated* or *flat tire* will flop under the rim as it rotates, leaving tire *flop marks*. In situations where air pressure is not lost rapidly, an underinflated tire mark may first appear and then lead into flop marks as all air pressure is lost.

7.029 *Bounce tire marks* are caused by a tire that is free to rotate, but that hits an uneven portion of roadway, e.g., pot hole, railway track, etc., and

Figure 7-26. Angled cross-tread abrasions indicate that the vehicle was sideslipping as in yaw.

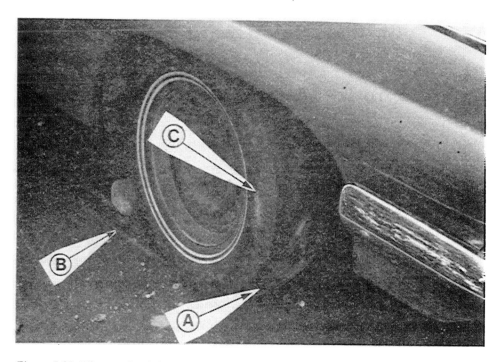

Figure 7-27. When a wheel skids or sideslips, striation or sideslip marks appear on the face of the tire, *A*, particularly when the skid or sideslip is on a gravel or gritty roadway surface. Matching or similar marks, *B*, will also occur to the roadway surface. If the force is great enough, the tire may roll or tuck under and the sidewall may come into contact with the roadway as indicated at *C*.

Figure 7-28. A skidding tire will have a cleaned or scraped area on that portion in contact with the roadway surface, as in *A*. If the tire skids over a gravel or gritty surface, striation marks may appear on the tread, as in *B*, and particles of the roadway surface may adhere to the tread surface, as in *C*.

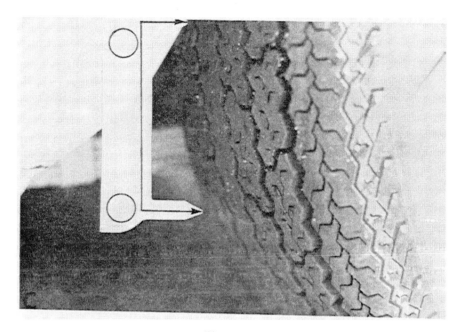

Figure 7-28 *C*.

Figure 7-29. A vehicle in a skid will drift to the lower side of a crowned or superelevated roadway, *B* to *C*. Note impending skid marks from *A* to *B* where braking is most effective.

Figure 7-30. A skidding tire will pick up debris, e.g., dirt, between its treads and deposit it where the wheel stops, *A* and *B*. This debris may be seen on the roadway after the vehicle again proceeds, but it is usually short-lived. This type of evidence is useful in determining where a vehicle stopped.

Figure 7-31. Burned off tire particles, *A* and *B*, are from a tire in a skid. These particles are short-lived evidence. Burned off tire particles appearing as a short, black streak in the center of skid mark, at *C*, were caused by a skidding tire striking sharp edge in pavement surface. Direction of travel is indicated by direction the dark streak leaves the sharp edge (Source: *Traffic Accident Investigators' Handbook* by Rivers. Courtesy Charles C Thomas, Publisher,

becomes airborne long enough for it to change its rotation. When it again strikes the roadway, very short skid marks result, usually about one foot (.3 meter) in length. Caution must be taken not to confuse bounce tire marks with skip skid marks. (*See also* Fig. 7-25.)

SKID AND SIDESLIP MARKS

7.030   Tires should be examined for indications of skidding or sliding. Crosswise striations on sides or tread face indicate that the tire was sliding sideways. Close examination may show that the striation marks are at an angle and resulted from the tire rotating and sideslipping at the same time, as when a vehicle is in yaw. A clean tire tread surface with longitudinal striations, which might appear very faint, indicate that the wheel was locked in a skid. The same tire area may have bits of tire tread scraped or rubbed off and particles of gravel embedded in the tread grooves. Often the tread face will have a *sandpaper* appearance when a skid is on a very hard, unpolished roadway surface such as portland

Figure 7-32. A locked or jammed wheel may leave a skid mark while being towed or moved. Caution must be taken not to confuse a skid mark caused in this manner with an accident skid mark, particularly after the vehicle is removed from the scene.

cement or when a pavement has particles of gravel or similar hard, gritty material on its surface.

7.031   An *impending skid mark* is that portion of a tire mark left by a braked wheel just before there is a complete cessation of rotation. Braking is most effective at this time. The mark left may appear as a cleaning action and will lead directly into a skid mark.[5]

7.032   The *end of a skid mark* may have a deposit of dirt or other substance on the pavement where the wheel stopped just before the point where it began to once again rotate. In soft surfaces, the end of a skid mark will have a mound of material pushed up ahead of where the tire stopped. (*See also* Fig. 7-16.)

SKID MARKS

7.033   A skid mark is a tire mark resulting from a locked wheel as a tire slides over a roadway or other surface. A wheel may become locked as the result of braking or from binding such as that which sometimes occurs during or as the result of collision. Skid marks are useful in determining:
>   a. Where a vehicle's brakes were applied
>   b. Minimum speed where the skid marks commenced
>   c. A vehicle's location on the roadway leading up to the point of collision
>   d. Point of collision
>   e. Path of travel before and after collision
>   f. Action of vehicle, e.g., rotation, change of direction
>   g. The number of wheels having braking capability

7.034   In normal *straight skids*, a properly inflated and loaded tire will leave a skid mark the width of the tire tread. The skid mark will have parallel tread rib marks. If the front wheels are turned or if the vehicle rotates or skids sideways so that a tire is not skidding straight ahead, the skid mark may appear wider than the tread width, depending upon the amount of tire tread in contact with the roadway. Under these circumstances, the parallel tread rib marks will not appear, but there may be some indication of rib marks caused by the ribs of a tire shoulder.

7.035   On bituminous concrete roadway surfaces, skid marks are caused by the smearing of the asphalt or tar of the surface mixture. This results from the heat generated by a skidding tire. Consequently, skid marks

Figure 7-33. Intermittent skid marks result from "pumping" the brake pedal with full application and release. Measure and add together each skid mark or set of skid marks for speed calculation purposes. (*See* paragraph 12.005(h).)

will be more apparent on this type of surface and may be visible for weeks. On hard surfaces such as cement or brick, skid marks appear as a cleaning action the width of the tire part that makes the mark. These types of marks are generally short-lived. In these cases, some tire smear or minute rubber particles may be found adhering to the roadway surface in the skid mark area because of the tire rubber melting or being scraped or rubbed off during the slide. These particles soon disappear as the result of wind action, passing vehicles, rain, etc. Skid marks on cold, bituminous concrete appear much the same as those on cement surfaces. (*See* Fig. 7-31.)

7.036   Skid marks are not usually left on wet pavement surfaces. This is because a moisture shield is formed between the tire and roadway surface that does not allow the normal friction heat to build up. Any skid mark that is left will normally soon disappear as the result of washing action by rain or passing vehicles. Similarly, any other type of tire mark on hard, wet surfaces is usually short-lived. As a tire passes over the surface, water is pushed to the sides and then rushes back to the tire path after the tire passes. A slight indication may remain for a short time but will rapidly disappear during rain.

7.037 In examining skid marks, the investigator should kneel down so that the eye level is approximately 24 inches (60 cm) above the roadway surface. When circumstances permit, a better view of skid marks may be had with the sun behind the investigator. Polarized sunglasses will provide a more clear view of skid marks during daylight.

7.038 When there is no evidence of braking from skid marks, the investigator should not assume on that basis alone that brakes were not applied. A vehicle equipped with an anti-skid braking system has braking capability without leaving skid marks. Therefore, the type of braking system should be checked. If a vehicle is equipped with an anti-skid braking system, evidence of any braking having taken place should be gathered from the driver, passengers or other witnesses, and resultant damages.

7.039 *Intermittent skid marks* are caused by intermittent brake applications and releases. The blank spaces are gaps between skid marks and are usually about 15 to 20 feet (5 to 6 meters), depending upon the speed of the vehicle at the time.

7.040 A *skip skid mark* is a braking skid mark interrupted at frequent regular intervals.[6] Skip skid marks occur when a wheel bounces on the roadway. The most commonly seen skip skid marks are caused by the braked rear wheels of an unloaded or lightly loaded semi-trailer. The gaps are usually about 3 feet (1 meter) in length. At the time of collision, the rear-end of a braking vehicle may bounce up, causing a skip skid mark. This is often useful in locating the point of impact. Also, when a locked wheel passes over a body or some other object, it may lift and bounce once or several times, leaving skip skid marks. Although skip skid marks are usually short, when a vehicle passes over an uneven portion of roadway, e.g., pot hole, railway track or a sharp, short incline, the gap may be much longer than 3 feet (1 meter).

7.041 When a pavement has particles of gravel, sand or similar hard, gritty material on its surface, a sliding tire will cause it to leave scratch marks on the roadway surface. Studded tires will leave scratches as well. These scratch or striation marks can occur on all types of hard surfaces. They will generally not be affected by wet surfaces, although they may not be readily visible until the surface dries. Such marks may be short-lived during rain.

Figure 7-34. A braked dual wheel of a lightly loaded or empty semi-trailer or other similar type of vehicle will often bounce, causing skip skid marks. For speed calculations, measure the overall distance, *A* to *B*, disregarding gaps. (*See* paragraph 12.005(g).)

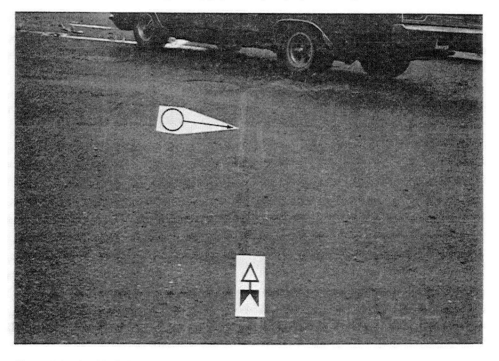

Figure 7-35. Studded tire skid mark. (Source: *Traffic Accident Investigators' Handbook* by Rivers. Courtesy Charles C Thomas, Publisher, Springfield, Illinois.)

7.042   A skidding vehicle will tend to slide or curve in the direction of the lower side of a superelevated or banked roadway. Because of a natural weight shift to the lower side, the skid marks on that side will often appear darker as the result of greater heat being generated. A curved skid mark will also occur when brakes do not lock or drag uniformly, such as when the brakes on one side lock before the other side. Such curves in skid marks should not be mistaken for results of steering action as steering a skidding vehicle has very little if any effect on the direction a vehicle will take. An exception to this, however, would be in the case of a truck-tractor unit that has either no front wheel brakes or front wheel brakes that are adjusted to prevent lock-up.

7.043   When brakes on a vehicle are applied and there is rapid deceleration, there is a sudden weight shift to the front and consequently onto the front tires. Because of this weight shift, the front-end dips and the rear-end rises. The additional weight on the front tires cause them to distort, similarly to an underinflated or overloaded tire, i.e., they tend to "cup." (*See* Fig. 8-15.) Most of the weight is carried on the front tires and as a result of the loss of weight on the rear tires, their treads tend to bulge or become oval in appearance similar to an overinflated tire. (*See* Fig.

Figure 7-36. Because of a forward shift in weight during braking action, front tires tend to "cup" in a similar manner to that of an overloaded tire with the greatest weight being carried on the outer edges. These edges leave dark parallel lines as at *A* and *B*. At the same time, the rear end lifts and the rear tires take on the shape of an overinflated tire with only the center of the tread touching the roadway surface as at *C*. In straight, overlapping skid marks, the rear tire skid marks will track inside the front tire skid marks as indicated by *C*.

8-15B). The skid mark of a rear tire will, consequently, be narrower in width than the actual tread face because the outer edges of the tread does not come into contact with the roadway. In a *straight, overlapping skid,* the rear tire skid marks will fall within the front tire skid marks. (*See* Fig. 7-36.)

7.044   A tire *scrub mark* is a tire mark resulting from a wheel that is locked or jammed during collision and moving on the roadway until such time as the vehicle stops or the wheel becomes free to rotate. The beginning of a scrub mark will often help in determining the point of impact.

7.045   When one vehicle collides with another vehicle or some other object, it may be suddenly pushed or directed to one side as the result of the opposing force. In these cases, if the vehicle is skidding up to the point of impact, the skid mark will become *offset* at the point of impact. This offset will, therefore, assist in establishing and in many cases establish the point of impact.

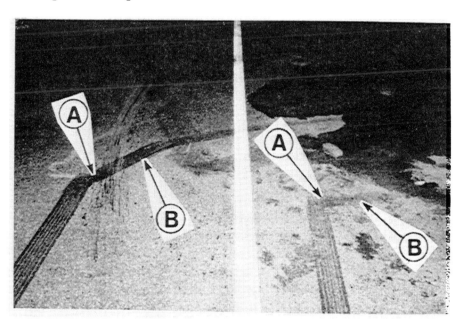

Figure 7-37. The point of impact may be established by following skid marks to *A* where tires dig into roadway surface because of downward thrust during collision causing a gouge, and then becoming offset causing a scrub mark, *B.*

Figure 7-38. A yaw mark begins as a thin, dark line caused by the outer edge of the front lead tire.

YAW AND SIDESLIP MARKS

7.046 A *scuff mark* is a friction mark on a pavement made by a tire that is both rotating and slipping: *acceleration scuffs, yaw marks, flat-tire marks.*[7]

7.047 A *yaw* or *sideslip* mark is caused by a rotating tire that is sideslipping. It appears on the roadway as a curved mark and is generally first caused by the lead front tire when a vehicle enters a curve at an excessive rate of speed. During a cornering maneuver, a vehicle's weight is shifted onto the lead front tire, which tends to roll under. The greatest weight is carried on the tire's outer edge. With this additional weight and the sideways thrust, tremendous heat is generated, which leaves a narrow, dark mark at its beginning (*see* Fig. 7-38) and widens as the vehicle goes into yaw (*see* Fig. 7-39) providing more tire contact with the roadway. A close examination of a yaw mark will reveal diagonal striation marks caused by the side of the tire tread as the tire sideslips.

7.048 Under normal circumstances, rotating rear tires track inside the front tires. However, when a vehicle goes into yaw, the rear tires tend to

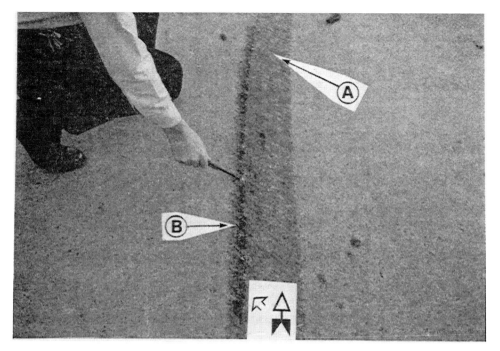

Figure 7-39. When a vehicle goes into yaw, a rotating, sideslipping tire will leave striation marks on the roadway surface, A. These marks are useful in determining the vehicle's direction of travel. A close examination will often reveal a dark, thin line at the outer lead edge of the yaw mark, similar to the beginning of a yaw mark, where the greatest heat is generated causing the asphalt or tar of the roadway surface to melt and smear, B.

Figure 7-40. When a vehicle rotates or goes into yaw, it will leave skid or sideslip marks of varying widths depending upon the positions of the tires in relation to the roadway. The position of a vehicle at various locations may be determined from these marks.

track outside the front tires. If the speed is great enough, the rear of the vehicle will slip sideways, causing the vehicle to go out of control, leave the roadway on a curve and/or possibly spin or overturn.

DEBRIS

7.049　*Debris* is loose material strewn on the road as the result of a traffic accident.[8] Debris can be solids or liquids including:
  a. Broken vehicle parts
  b. Fluids, e.g., radiator water, anti-freeze, motor oil
  c. Underbody debris, e.g., vehicle undercoating, road tar, dirt, mud, sand
  d. Cargo being carried on a vehicle
  e. Vehicle paint or rust
  f. Blood from pedestrian, driver or passenger, or domestic or wild animal

7.050　It is important to establish whether certain things were actually deposited where they are found because of the collision or whether they were moved there afterwards by some person at the scene. Some debris, particularly underbody debris, will fall at or close to the point of impact. Other debris, e.g., hub caps, bottles, etc., may bounce and roll considerable distances before coming to rest. Vehicle doors, seats, windshield glass and other similar items may be strewn around the accident area by bystanders in an effort to rescue victims inside a vehicle.

7.051　Caution must be taken to properly identify oil and grease found on the roadway. For example, if power steering fluid were identified as brake fluid, brake failure could be mistakenly considered a cause or contributing factor in an accident.

7.052　The manner in which debris is scattered will assist the investigator in determining a vehicle's direction of travel at the time of impact and the point of impact. Liquid debris, particularly, will often establish a vehicle's path of travel after impact and the place where the vehicle came to rest or final position.

7.053　When debris falls from a vehicle during impact, it falls forward unless otherwise deflected. Underbody debris, for example, will fall forward in a heap or pile close to the point of impact and spread out in a fan-like pattern becoming more thinly spread as it gains distance.

Figure 7-41. A vehicle's path after collision may be traced from water or oil trails caused by the release of liquids from such parts as the radiator or transmission case. By following back along these trails from a vehicle's resting place, the approximate point of collision may often be established.

7.054 When a collision breaks a radiator, the pressure within forces the coolant out immediately. Initially the coolant will *spatter* out onto the roadway as *scattered drops*. After the pressure has subsided, the coolant will *dribble* out, and if the vehicle is moving, the dribble will form a *trail* on the roadway. When a vehicle is at rest, the liquid will dribble out to form a *puddle* or *pool*. If a puddle or pool is not absorbed quickly into the surface, there may be *runoff* in the form of rills or small streams. This type of evidence is very helpful in establishing the point of impact and a vehicle's path of travel to its final position after the point of impact. The investigator must examine the scene immediately for evidence of fluid stains such as water and gasoline, as they may disappear quickly because of their evaporation qualities. (*See* Fig. 7-1.)

REFERENCES

1. Rivers, R.W.: *Traffic Accident Investigators' Handbook.* Charles C Thomas, Springfield, Illinois, 1980, p. 119.
2. Rivers, R.W.: *Traffic Accident Investigators' Handbook.* Charles C Thomas, Springfield, Illinois, 1980, p. 119.
3. Baker, J. Stannard: *Traffic Accident Investigation Manual.* Traffic Institute, Northwestern University, Evanston, Illinois, 1975, p. 320.
4. Rivers, R.W.: *Traffic Accident Investigators' Handbook.* Charles C Thomas, Springfield, Illinois, 1980, p. 29.
5. Rivers, R.W.: *Traffic Accident Investigators' Handbook.* Charles C Thomas, Springfield, Illinois, 1980, p. 29.
6. Baker, J. Stannard: *Traffic Accident Investigation Manual.* Traffic Institute, Northwestern University, Evanston, Illinois, 1975, p. 320.
7. Baker, J. Stannard: *Traffic Accident Investigation Manual.* Traffic Institute, Northwestern University, Evanston, Illinois, 1975, p. 319.
8. Baker, J. Stannard: *Traffic Accident Investigation Manual.* Traffic Institute, Northwestern University, Evanston, Illinois, 1975, p. 315.

Chapter 8

VEHICLE MECHANICAL INSPECTION

8.001   A thorough vehicle mechanical inspection should be carried out at the accident scene. Emphasis must be placed on all parts and systems that might have caused or contributed to the accident. These elements include such things as the accelerator being pressed by the driver to put the vehicle in motion, the various functions and maneuvers involved during the trip, e.g., steering, signalling turns, etc., through to the brake application made in an effort to stop the vehicle.

8.002   A vehicle may be found to have numerous defects, malfunctions and damaged parts. It is essential that an inspection determine whether or not these contributed in any way to the accident cause, bearing in mind that they could have resulted from the collision rather than being a prior condition.

8.003   A more thorough vehicle inspection may be carried out later at a more suitable and convenient location. This follow-up examination should be with a view of determining the condition and operational efficiency and effectiveness of such items as:
   a. Brake linings
   b. Wheel cylinders
   c. Fluid pressures (p.s.i.) in brake and power steering lines
   d. Mechanical defects that came about as the result of age, misuse, normal wear or poor maintenance
   e. Mechanical defects related to the manufacturer's design or assembly
   f. Improper or incorrect repair made by repair stations, e.g., garages
   g. Internal examination of tires and such

EXPERT EXAMINATION

8.004   Professional traffic accident reconstructionists are able to apply scientific principles to data and other evidence gathered during field investigations.[1] Where the need for an in-depth inspection or analysis is indicated, such items as braking systems, oils found on the roadway (e.g., brake or steering fluids), lamp filaments and broken metal parts possibly resulting from metal fatigue should be preserved. They can then be subjected to scientific examination or analysis by those who can give expert testimony, such as a professional accident reconstructionist, mechanical engineer or laboratory technician.

MECHANICAL INSPECTION

8.005   A mechanical inspection should include all of the following.

Vehicle Description

Obtain a complete description of the vehicle for identification and other investigational purposes, including:
   a. License plate number
   b. State or Province
   c. Owner's name and address
   d. Registration number
   e. Make, year, model/type and color
   f. Serial number (VIN)
   g. Insurance particulars

Accelerator

Examine the accelerator system both visually and manually. Make observations for worn parts and any indication of scraping, rubbing or wear that might indicate binding in the linkage system. The condition of the pedal tread should be noted as this might have a bearing on the amount of adhesion between the driver's shoe sole and the accelerator pedal. Depress and release the accelerator pedal several times to check for freedom of movement, retrieval and any indication of malfunction.

Brake System

If brake failure is indicated, check the roadway leading up to the point of collision for evidence of brake fluid loss on roadway surface. If there was leakage and brakes were applied, spurts of oil will have been forced out of the brake lines onto the roadway. The point of collision should be examined for evidence that would indicate that brake lines were broken and any fluid loss resulted from the damage caused during collision.

Examine fluid level in the master cylinder. Inspect all fluid lines and connections from the master cylinder to all wheels. Check the inner side of wheels for fluid stains. Stains might be an indication that the wheel cylinder was leaking.

If there is low brake pedal reserve, pump the brake pedal to determine how many strokes are required to restore brake to full or normal brake pedal. Low brake pedal reserve may be a cause of delayed braking.

Damp brake linings can cause braking deficiency. When there is evidence of brake maladjustment, fading or hard pedal effort, examine tires and wheel brake drums for dampness, and examine roadway leading up to the accident area for water. A later examination may be made for oil or grease on brake linings, which can have a similar effect.

Extensive braking on long, steep hills, particularly in the case of large commercial vehicles, may cause brake linings to overheat, resulting in fading or total loss of braking efficiency.

On-scene brake system examination should include:
  a. *Type of braking system*
     • hydraulic
     • power assist
     • air
  b. *Anti-locking device.* If the vehicle is equipped with a locking device, it should be noted whether the device is on all wheels.
  c. *Adjustment* (Locking uniformity). Improper wheel brake adjustment may cause a vehicle to swerve to one side or the other.
  d. *Master cylinder.* Check fluid level in master cylinder. Low level fluid may impair braking response. Low fluid level may be caused by leaks in fluid lines, defective seals or damaged cylinder body.
  e. *Brake pedal and pedal linkage.* Broken rods or fasteners can result in total brake failure or impaired braking response.
  f. *Parking brake.* An inspection of the parking brake system is particularly important in park-runaway accidents. A broken cable or missing fasteners can allow a vehicle to roll on inclines. Ratchet slippage will release the brake, allowing the vehicle to roll.
  g. *Pedal tread.* Pedal tread should be examined for wear and dampness caused by water, oil or grease, which might result in a shoe slipping off the pedal. The type of shoe sole should also be examined in an effort to determine the amount of adhesiveness there would be between the shoe sole and pedal tread.

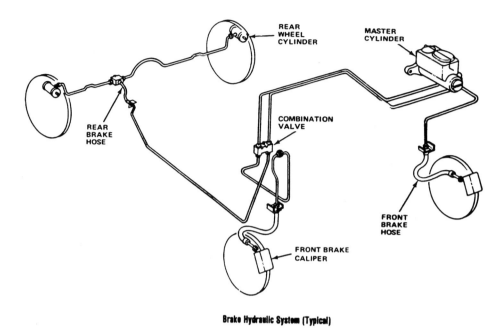

Brake Hydraulic System (Typical)

Figure 8-1. Typical hydraulic brake system. (Courtesy American Motors (Canada) Limited, Brampton, Ontario.)

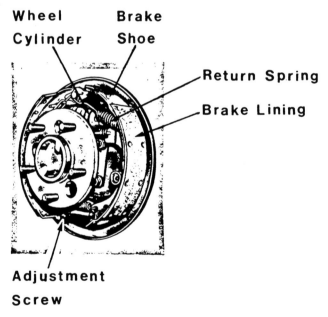

Figure 8-2. Brake wheel assembly. (Source: *Traffic Accident Investigators' Handbook* by Rivers. Courtesy Charles C Thomas, Publisher, Springfield, Illinois.)

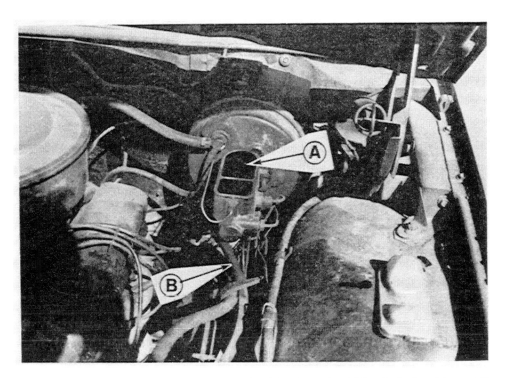

Figure 8-3. Hydraulic brake system *reservoir* fluid level (*A*) should be checked and hoses (*B*) should be examined for leakage.

Figure 8-4. Fluid stains on inside of wheel indicates that wheel cylinder may be leaking. (Source: *Traffic Accident Investigators' Handbook* by Rivers. Courtesy Charles C Thomas, Publisher, Springfield, Illinois.)

h. *Lines* (fluid, vacuum, air). Examine lines and fittings from the master cylinder through to all wheels. Broken lines may result in no braking capability. Leakage may result in impaired braking efficiency or total braking loss.

i. *Pedal Reserve.* Inadequate pedal reserve may result from low fluid level in master cylinder. Loss of pedal reserve can be caused by broken brake arm or separation of linkage. Low pedal reserve can result in impaired braking efficiency or total braking loss. Broken brake arm or separation of linkage can result in total loss of braking capability.

j. *Air-brake Systems.* On-scene air-brake system examination should include:
   • Reservoir pressure
   • Chamber push-rod travel
   • Condition of lines and connections
   • Audible air leaks

k. *Power Assist System.* A power assisted steering system should be checked for:
   • Broken or disconnected hoses
   • Tension of drive belt for breakage or slippage
   • Fluid level of pump reservoir

Vehicle Damage

Body damage can give an indication as to the direction of travel of vehicles involved and in some instances the approximate speed. Previous mechanical damage may cause a malfunction resulting in an accident, e.g., bent tie-rod becoming broken during travel causing loss of steering control. Defective door latches may allow a door to open, resulting in a driver or passenger being thrown from a vehicle. Corroded or rusted floor pan or other body part may permit exhaust fumes to enter driver's compartment, resulting in carbon-monoxide poisoning. A damaged or broken frame or cross-member can cause misalignment resulting in impairment of steering response or loss of steering control. A broken or defective hood latch may allow hood to spring open, obstructing the driver's vision.

Particular attention should be given to any indication that an occupant struck the inside parts of a vehicle. This includes such areas as the windshield, dash, control knobs, etc. This information may be used later

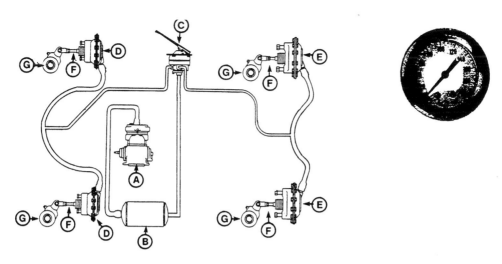

Figure 8-5. Typical air brake system. The compressor (*A*) pumps air to the reservoir (*B*). Once the foot valve (*C*) is depressed, air flows under pressure to the front and rear brake chambers (*D* and *E*). Brake chamber push rods (*F*) move the slack adjusters (*G*), which rotate the brake cams (*See* Fig. 8-6), forcing the brake shoes against the drums causing friction to stop the vehicle. If slack adjusters are not properly adjusted, brakes may be ineffective. A pressure gauge is usually mounted on the dashboard in the cab. Observations of the gauge during full brake application will assist the investigator in determining whether or not the system is operating at and maintaining required air pressure. (Source: *The British Columbia Air Brake Manual* (undated). Published by the British Columbia Motor Vehicle Branch, Victoria, B.C., Canada.)

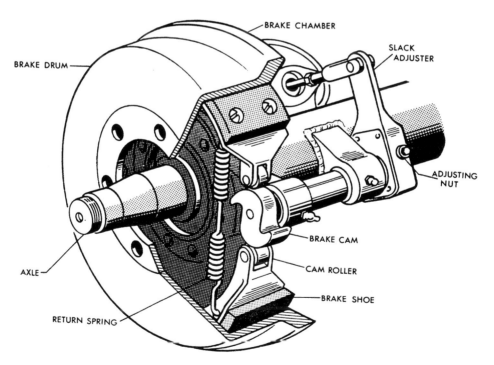

Figure 8-6. Air brake wheel assembly (Source: *The British Columbia Air Brake Manual* (undated) Published by the British Columbia Motor Vehicle Branch, Victoria, B.C., Canada).

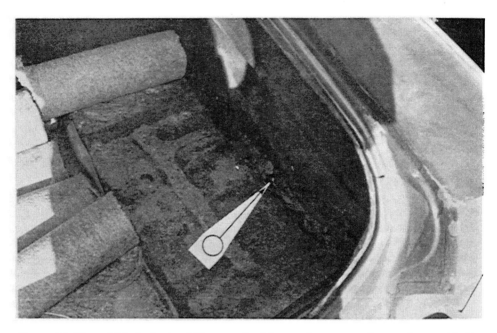

Figure 8-7. The vehicle body should be examined for erosion or rusted areas that would allow carbon monoxide to enter the driver's or passengers' compartment.

to determine seating positions and how an occupant received certain injuries.

Exhaust System

The exhaust system, including emission control devices, should be examined from the manifold through to the end of the tail-pipe for corrosion, holes, damage or defects that would allow exhaust leakage. Any leakage should be related to the possibility of the exhaust fumes entering the driver's compartment that, in turn, could have caused carbon-monoxide poisoning.

Gear Shift Lever

The gear shift lever position will assist in determining the direction of travel (forward or reverse) and corroboration for speed estimates. It should be borne in mind, however, that the lever could have been forced to its position during the collision.

Horn

The ability of the horn to give an audible signal should be examined. A defective horn will not allow a driver to audibly indicate a warning to other drivers and pedestrians. The type of switch, e.g., ring, button, shroud or spoke, and the type of horn, e.g., electrical vacuum or air, should be noted.

Lights

Oncoming drivers can be temporarily blinded by oncoming headlights that are improperly adjusted. Similarly, improper adjustment may not give a driver a clear view of the roadway for a sufficient distance. This can result in a driver "overdriving" his headlights, i.e., his speed might be too great for the distance he is able to see, thereby not giving him time to stop upon perceiving a hazard. A heavy load on the rear of a vehicle will raise the headlight projection giving the same effect as being adjusted too high. A misaligned rear axle will direct the headlights to either one side or the other, which will impair a driver's vision of the opposite side of the roadway.

Check the condition of *hazard warning lights* and whether they were in operation in all accidents involving parked or stalled vehicles.

The position and color of reflectors and clearance lights should be examined, particularly in nighttime accidents. Whether or not large commercial type vehicles had side reflectors is very important in intersection accidents.

Check the condition and position of all light switches. Note the position of the high-beam or dimmer switch and high-beam indicator light in all accidents where headlights might have been a factor. Check brake lights, which can be a factor in rear-end collisions. Signal light switch position and indicator light should be examined in all accidents involving turns. Determine how back-up light is switched on, i.e., manually or automatically, by changing into reverse gear.

Loads

The manner in which loads are carried can affect the safe operation of a vehicle. Improperly placed loads may obstruct a driver's control over the steering wheel or his view of the highway. If a vehicle is improperly loaded, particularly high loads, the center of mass may be placed so high that the vehicle will overturn; or, if the center of mass is too far to the rear, the driver will lose control of the steering.

Mirrors

Check the location and positioning of inside and outside mirrors. Make an examination of the view afforded the driver from his seated position. Mirror positioning is very important in pull-out and sideswipe and backing up accidents.

Power Train

Examine motor mounts, drive-shaft and drive-shaft linkages. A broken drive-shaft may drop and dig into the roadway, throwing the vehicle out of control.

Safety Restraint Systems

Personal injuries in motor vehicle accidents are often related to whether a vehicle was equipped with a safety restraint system. An investigator should determine whether the vehicle was equipped and if so its condition and whether or not the restraint system was used.

The most common safety restraint systems are (a) seat belt and (b) air bag systems.

There are obvious indicators in establishing whether or not seat lap belts were used. Some of these are:

BELT NOT WORN*

1. Belts defeated by buckling together in front of, behind, or under seat.
2. Shoulder belt stowed (in pre-1974 cars).
3. Belts not accessible, e.g., pushed down behind seat.
4. Sometimes car deformation intrudes and outboard anchorage is compressed against seat. If belt was worn, could it have retracted? If not, and it is not visible, probably it was not worn.
5. If there is a windshield impact—spider web pattern and bulge— *suspects* non-use.
6. If steering wheel is damaged by occupant, *suspects* non-use.
7. If upper dashboard (instrument panel) is damaged by occupant, *suspect* non-use.

---

*(*Source:* Marion Oversby, Co-ordinator, Traffic Accident Research Unit, B.C. Research. Report dated June 2, 1977).

8. If occupant is ejected, suspect non-use (*or* incorrect belt wearing).
9. Check injury diagnosis—see below.

BELT WORN

1. Belts jammed in "out" position due to side intrusion, preventing belt retracting.
2. Belt webbing cut to release occupant (check by whom cut).
3. Occupant retained in original seating position and probably less injured than one might think (given the accident severity).
4. Check injury diagnosis—people wearing *lap and shoulder* belts show decreased likelihood of head injury. Belt associated injuries— from shoulder belt—rib fractures, sternal fracture, clavicle fracture, seat belt bruises on chest and abdomen. When the torso is restrained, limbs are still mobile—often bruised shins (from beneath dashboard, steering column, etc.) Usually absence of facial injury pain (neck and back) are common complaints.
5. Check belts for signs of stretching under extreme force.

Air Bags

An investigation of an air bag systems should determine if the air bag deployed as the result of the collision or if it deployed without an apparent cause, thereby contributing to the cause of the accident. Such an examination should be carried out by an experienced investigator or someone knowledgeable in air bag installations. There are various types of air bag systems in use and there presently appears to be no singular approach that can be recommended in terms of determining whether or not there was faulty deployment. Because of inherent dangers, caution must always be taken during an air bag inspection or investigation to prevent injury to the investigator or others. Such examinations are beyond the scope of this manual and its intended level of training. Unless properly qualified to examine air bag deployment causes, the investigator should call upon the services of a properly qualified person to conduct such an examination.

Steering and Suspension Systems

An effective examination of steering and suspension systems can be made if the vehicle is lifted by a tow-truck.

An on-scene steering and suspension examination should include a check of all parts that could contribute to the loss of steering or vehicle control including shock absorbers, springs, control arms and torsion bars, and any indication that the frame, suspension or steering mechanism had been altered.

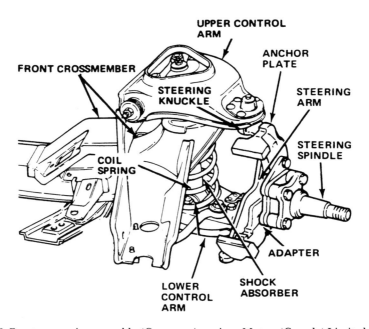

Figure 8-8. Front suspension assembly (Courtesy American Motors (Canada) Limited, Brampton, Ontario).

To examine the general condition of the steering system, turn the steering wheel fully to one side and then to the other, and then back-and-forth in quick, short turns. Such maneuvers will often indicate whether the system has worn or loose parts. Examine the system for continuity from the steering wheel through to each front wheel. Also, make a visual examination for loose mountings and worn or binding parts. Power assisted steering systems should also be checked for broken or disconnected hoses, pump reservoir fluid level, and slippage or breakage of drive belts.

Sunvisors

Check for the presence of sunvisors, their condition and positions, particularly as they might have related to a driver's view being obscured by bright sunlight.

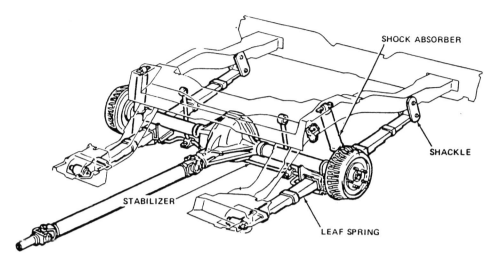

Figure 8-9. Leaf spring rear suspension system (Courtesy General Motors of Canada Limited, Oshawa, Ontario)

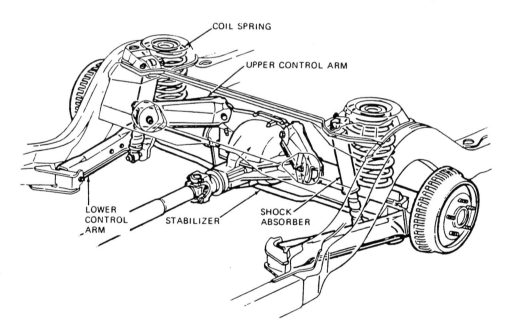

Figure 8-10. Coil rear suspension system. (Courtesy General Motors of Canada Limited, Oshawa, Ontario.)

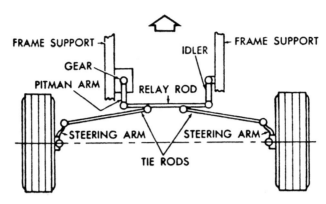

Figure 8-11. Steering linkage (Courtesy General Motors of Canada Limited, Oshawa, Ontario).

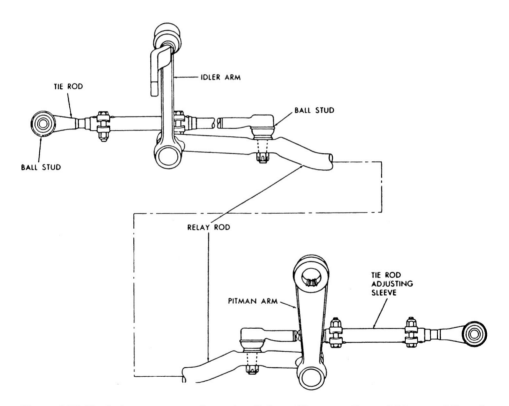

Figure 8-12. Typical components of steering linkage (Courtesy General Motors of Canada Limited, Oshawa, Ontario).

Figure 8-13. A power steering unit inspection should include an examination of the hydraulic pump (*A*), fluid level (*B*), drive belt (*C*), and hoses (*D*).

Tires

When a tire failure is possible or is suspected, an inspection should include a complete description of the tire covering its limitations, maintenance, general condition, amount and pattern of tread wear and any indication of damage or blow-out. Where damage is evident, the inspection should determine:

  a. *Type,* e.g., caused by rock, glass fragments, metal protrusion as result of impact, etc.
  b. *Location* related to serial number or other tire identification mark
  c. *Location* related to rim damage
  d. *Location* related to damaged vehicle parts that might have caused the tire damage.

The highway leading up to the point of collision should be examined for tire fragments or tire marks that would indicate prior tire failure and possibly the cause for the failure, e.g., rocks, glass fragments, etc.

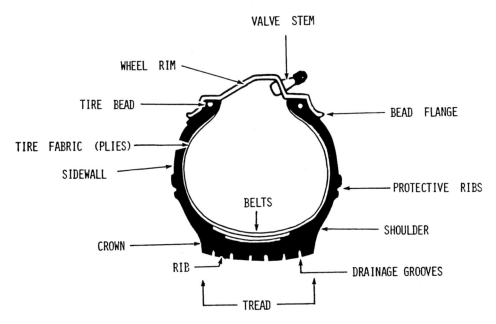

Figure 8-14. Parts of a tire.

Check to determine whether or not all tires are compatible. Because of their fuller tread contact with the roadway, particularly in cornering, a mix of radial type tires and bias type tires can result in loss of steering control.

There are three types of tire construction currently in use. They are referred to as bias-ply, bias-belted, and radial ply construction. The description for each construction type is derived from the method used to position the tire body cord plies in relation to the centerline of the tread.

BIAS–PLY TIRE CONSTRUCTION

Bias-ply tires are constructed with the body cord plies extending from bead-to-bead at an angle to the centerline of the tread (*See* Fig. 8-18). Alternate plies overlap one another at opposing angles.

BIAS–BELTED TIRE CONSTRUCTION

Bias-belted tires are constructed basically the same as bias-ply tires. However, in addition to the angled body cord plies, they also have belts that encircle the tire. These belts are located under the tire tread and extend from tread shoulder to tread shoulder (*See* Fig. 8-18).

RADIAL–PLY TIRE CONSTRUCTION

Radial-ply tires, like bias-belted tires, also have belts under the tread

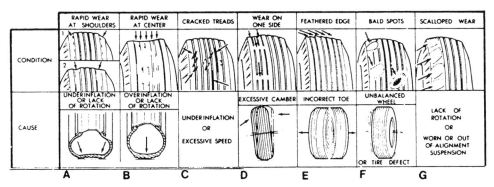

	RAPID WEAR AT SHOULDERS	RAPID WEAR AT CENTER	CRACKED TREADS	WEAR ON ONE SIDE	FEATHERED EDGE	BALD SPOTS	SCALLOPED WEAR
CONDITION							
CAUSE	UNDERINFLATION OR LACK OF ROTATION	OVERINFLATION OR LACK OF ROTATION	UNDERINFLATION OR EXCESSIVE SPEED	EXCESSIVE CAMBER	INCORRECT TOE	UNBALANCED WHEEL OR TIRE DEFECT	LACK OF ROTATION OR WORN OR OUT OF ALIGNMENT SUSPENSION
	A	B	C	D	E	F	G

Figure 8-15. Tire wear patterns. (Courtesy American Motors (Canada) Limited, Brampton, Ontario.) *A.* Underinflated tire: Note "cupping" of tire tread at its point of contact with roadway surface, and subsequent wear at the outer edges of the tread. Similar distortion takes place when a tire is overloaded and to front tires when there is a forward weight shift during hard braking. Under extreme acceleration, rear tires will also distort in a similar manner. *B.* Overinflated tire: Note bulging of tire tread at its point of contact with roadway surface, and subsequent wear at the center of the tread. Similar distortion takes place with rear tires during rapid braking when the vehicle's rear end raises because of a forward weight shift.

Figure 8-16. An investigator must not confuse a flat tire caused by damage incurred during collision with a flat tire that may have been a contributing factor in the accident. A flat tire before collision will, in most instances, leave flat tire marks on the roadway surface before point of impact. In this case, although the tire tread is badly worn, air pressure loss was caused by a broken body part cutting the tire tread and casing during collision. It is very important to match such damage with the part that caused it.

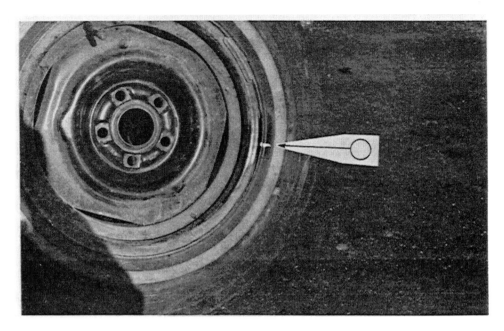

Figure 8-17. Before removing a tire from the tire rim, both should be marked in such a manner as to make it possible to relate damages after the tire is removed.

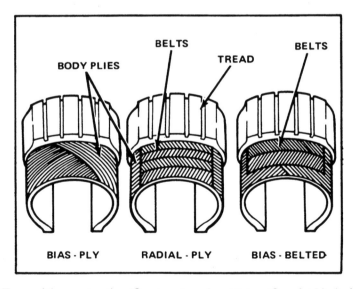

Figure 8-18. Types of tire construction (Courtesy American Motors (Canada) Limited, Brampton, Ontario).

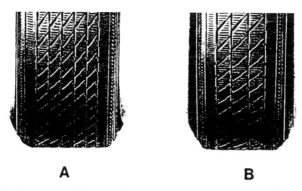

A　　　　　**B**

Figure 8-19. Radial type tire (A) gives the appearance of an underinflated tire except that it maintains full tread-roadway contact. (B) represents a properly inflated standard type tire, e.g., bias-ply. Source: British Rubber Manufacturers' Association Limited, London. Brochure (undated).

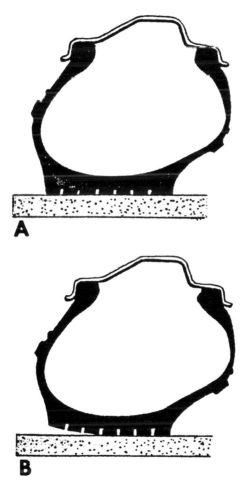

Figure 8-20. In cornering, the slip angle of a radial tire is practically eliminated (A) and the tread stays in a flat, full contact position with the roadway surface. Because of this, a radial tire reacts in a positive way to steering. The sidewall of a bias-type tire curls and tucks under and the inside of the tread lifts (B) when driven into a curve at high speed. Steering becomes difficult. Because of their individual and unique characteristics, radial and other types of tires should not be mixed.

Figure 8-21. Tire tread wear indicator.

that encircle the tire and extend from tread shoulder to tread shoulder. However, these tires are constructed with the body cord plies at right angles to the centerline of the tread. The plies cross the tread centerline at an angle of approximately 90 degrees (*See* Fig. 8-18). Because the body cord plies radiate from the tread centerline, this type of construction is designated radial-ply.[2]

TIRE MAINTENANCE AND CONDITION

A number of jurisdictions have statutes governing minimum allowable tread depths. A visible check of tire wear may be made by examining a tire for *tread wear indicators,* which are molded into the bottom of the tread grooves. The tire should be replaced when these indicator bands become visible (*See* Fig. 8-21).

Wheels

Check wheels for damage or defects, e.g., fractures, defective welds; improperly installed, missing, loose or worn studs, and worn (elongated) mounting holes. Wheel damage and improper fitting or missing studs can contribute to the loss of vehicle control.

Figure 8-22. Contact windshield damage will show radial cracks (*A*) and circular cracks (*B*) in glass.

Examine the inside of rear wheels and tires for presence of oil, which might have leaked from a wheel cylinder. This would indicate possible brake deficiency or failure.

Windshield and Windows

Examine the conditions of windows and the windshield for view obstructions such as dirt, dust, ice, snow, decals, banners, cracks, stone bruises, etc., that would impair a driver's clear view of the highway ahead, behind and to the side. Damaged glass can cause glare from headlights or other bright lights impairing a driver's vision.

Note whether side windows are closed, partially closed or fully open. This evidence might be important in cases where a driver states that he did not hear a horn or other warning device, e.g., siren, or when there is a possibility that an object such as an insect entered the vehicle causing driver distraction.

Figure 8-23. Contact damage with a spider-web pattern and an outward bulge indicates that the contact was made from the inside of the vehicle. This type of contact damage is common when a driver's or passenger's head strikes a windshield during collision. A person's injuries suffered in this manner will assist in determining seating arrangements of occupants.

Figure 8-24. Impact windshield damage caused by a stone.

Figure 8-25. Induced windshield damage caused by an indirect force. This type of force usually makes at least two sets of parallel cracks crossing each other in a checkerboard fashion.

Windshield Wipers and Defrosters

Examine the condition and efficiency of the windshield wiper and defrosting or defogging devices. The type of windshield wiper should also be noted, e.g., electrical, vacuum or mechanical. Check the condition of the wiper blades and blade arms. Damaged, deteriorated or improperly adjusted wiper blade arms can cause inadequate wiper blade contact with the glass, resulting in impaired driver vision. If the defrosting or defogging devices are not functional, the driver may have wiped the frost or fog from the windshield thereby losing control of the steering. The switch positions for these devices should be checked to determine whether they were in the "on" or "off" position.

ITEM	FINDINGS, EXPLANATIONS CONCLUSIONS AND COMMENTS

Vehicle Description

Owner's Name
Owner's Address
License plate no.
State or Province
Registration no.
Make
Year
Model/Type
Color
Serial no. (VIN)
Odometer reading

Liability Insurance

Company
Address
Policy no.
Policy period
Agent
Agent's address

Air-Conditioning Unit

Position of control (i.e., on or off)
Defects (e.g., drawing in exhaust fumes)

Accelerator

Freedom of movement
Linkage
Pedal tread
Retrieval (spring)

Damage to Vehicle

Location
Estimated amount

Brakes

Type
• air
• hydraulic
• power assist

Figure 8-26. Vehicle inspection guide.

ITEM

Anti-Skid Device
• 2 wheel
• 4 wheel
• not equipped
Emergency braking device
Hand brake
Lines (fluid, vacuum, air)
• collision damage
• cracked
• leaks
• rock fracture
• worn
Locking uniformity
Master cylinder
Pedal tread
• good condition
• worn
Master cylinder
• fluid level

Doors

Manual or Power
Handles
Latches
Safety catches
General operation (e.g., jammed closed, hinge
 separation, etc.)

Exhaust Systema

Connections
Exhaust pipe
Manifold connection
Muffler
Tail-pipe

Fire Damage

Origin
• engine compartment
• fuel tank area
• passenger compartment
• trunk
• other

Figure 8-26 continued.

ITEM

FINDINGS, EXPLANATIONS
CONCLUSIONS AND COMMENTS

Frame
"A" frame
Cross members
Frame, general
Collision damage

Gear Shift Lever

Location
Position (i.e., 1st, 2nd gear, etc.)

Horn

Type (e.g., electrical, vacuum, air)
Audibility
Switch type (e.g., ring, button, shroud, spoke)

Lights

Lights, general (e.g., type, color, number, loca-
    tion and condition)
• back-up
• brake
• clearance
• fog
• hazard warning
• headlights
• high-beam indicator
• signal
• signal light indicator
• tail-lights
Switches and their positions (e.g., on or off,
    etc.)
• back-up light
• brake-light
• headlight
• headlight dimmer
• signal light

Mirrors

Location
Position
Type

Figure 8-26 continued.

ITEM

FINDINGS, EXPLANATIONS
CONCLUSIONS AND COMMENTS

Power Train
Broken drive shaft, etc. Note any contact with
   roadway.

Reflectors

Reflectors, general (e.g., type, color,
   number, locations and condition).

Safety Equipment

Head restraints
Seat belt restraints
Air bags
Flags, flares, fuses
Other

Speedometer

General condition
Reading in miles or kilometers

Steering

Ball joints
Drag links
Idler arm
King pins
Linkage, general
Steering-box
Steering wheel freeplay
Tie rods
Type (e.g., manual power)

Steering Wheel

Damage
Occupant contact

Suspension
Control arms
Shocks
Springs
Torsion bars

Figure 8-26 continued.

ITEM	FINDINGS, EXPLANATIONS CONCLUSIONS AND COMMENTS

Tires

Make
Name
Ply
Load capacity
Serial no.
Construction type (e.g., radial, bias-ply,
   bias-belted) Note any mix of tire type.
Sidewall type
Size
Pressure
 • recommended
 • actual
Tube or tubeless
Tread type (e.g., summer, winter, etc.)
Tread wear (e.g., great, light, medium)
Tread wear pattern
 • sides
 • center
 • uneven
Tread depth
 • new
 • percent worn
Recap
Chains
Studded
Damage
 • type (e.g., blow-out, cut, puncture, abrasions,
   etc.)
 • location related to serial number
 • location related to rim damage
 • location related to vehicle damage
General condition

Wheels

Condition, general
Rim
Lugs (e.g., missing, loose, worn)
Damage (i.e., type and location)

Figure 8-26 continued.

ITEM	FINDINGS, EXPLANATIONS CONCLUSIONS AND COMMENTS
Windshield and Windows Clear Tinted View obstructions Damage (including occupant contact) Windows and Vents • open • partially open • closed General condition *Windshield Wipers* Type (e.g., mechanical, vacuum, electrical) Blades and blade arms Switch • condition • on or off position *Windshield and Window Defrosters* Type Switch • condition • on or off position General condition	

Figure 8-26 continued.

REFERENCES

1. Rivers, R.W.: *Traffic Accident Investigator's Handbook.* Charles C Thomas, Springfield, Illinois, 1980, p. 29.
2. American Motors (Canada) Limited: *1979 Technical Service Manual AMC* (A791001). American Motors (Canada) Limited, Brampton, Ontario, Canada, 1979, p.2G1.

Chapter 9

PHOTOGRAPHY

9.001 A photograph, properly taken, conveys a true representation of the scene to the viewer. A picture helps solve the questions of what, where, how, and why an accident happened for courts of law and others who have an interest in traffic accident investigations. Photographs should, however, complement comprehensive notes and measurements, not replace.

9.002 Use good photographic equipment, know how to use the equipment properly and use proper photographic techniques. If the investigator is not fully familiar with accident photography, he should have someone with the necessary expertise take photographs for him. When someone else takes the photographs, the investigator should advise that person what photographs to take.

9.003 Be able to identify pictures. Record the following minimum information when photographs are taken:
   a. Date and time
   b. Place
   c. Case heading
   d. Case file number
   e. Photographer's name
   f. Witnesses' names, if available
   g. Camera positions in relation to those things being photographed.

9.004 First, decide what pictures are required. Take several pictures. It will then be possible to select the best single picture. The best single picture records the most useful information and shows the relationships between all things required in a picture to adequately and accurately depict the scene.

9.005 Photographs must be properly taken so as to not distort the facts. Do not tilt the camera. If the camera is tilted, for example, a hill will look steeper than it actually is. Taking photographs from an improper height

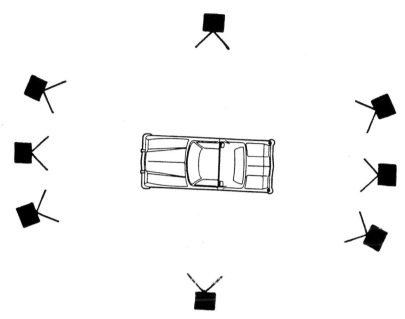

Figure 9-1. Camera positions. Photographs should be taken of both sides, front end and rear end of vehicle to show damage or lack of damage and damage location. Additional photographs, including close-ups, should be taken to show damage detail. Overhead pictures are helpful in matching up damages between vehicles. (Source: *Traffic Accident Investigators' Handbook* by Rivers. Courtesy Charles C Thomas, Publisher, Springfield, Illinois.)

or angle could give the impression that an obstruction such as a fence or hedge obstructed the view of a driver when in fact it did not have a detrimental effect on a driver's ability to see another vehicle.

9.006 Take photographs parallel to and at right angles to the roadway, showing the relationships of the various points being photographed to the edge of the roadway, center lines, roadway defects, stop-signs, traffic-control devices, etc.

9.007 Take photographs so as to depict the scene as the drivers would have seen it. Include in these, if possible, photographs taken while seated in the vehicle or ones similar to them, holding the camera at eye level.

9.008 Photographs should be taken from a distance showing the scene and a general view of terrain and surrounding areas. These should be followed by photographs taken from the point of possible perception, the point of actual perception, the point of no escape and other areas of the series of events in order to show what the drivers would have seen as they approached the point of impact. Also photograph vehicles in various

Figure 9-2. An investigator must know how to use his camera equipment properly. Improper camera settings can, for example, render a photograph useless.

positions to show their visibility to another driver as he approached the point of impact. These positions should include the *series of events* positions.

9.009   Photograph short-lived evidence, e.g., water trails, tire prints, skid marks, blood and other things that might be moved, destroyed or lost, as soon as possible. Their locations may be marked for purposes of taking additional photographs and measurements later in the investigation.

9.010   Take *medium close-up* views of specific damages and other evidence requiring particular photographic detail. These photographs should be taken close enough to give descriptive detail of the object and yet have enough surrounding area included to relate it to the general area. *Close-up* photographs should also be taken when minute detail of evidence is required.

9.011   Identifying markers and/or rulers or tapes may be placed alongside or in such a position as to better explain positions or measurements of certain types of evidence, e.g., tire marks, chips, gouges, etc. When photographing a tire mark, place a well-marked ruler beside the mark so

Figure 9-3. An investigator must be able to explain all marks and all things that appear in a photograph such as shadows, which might be mistaken for skid marks.

Figure 9-4. A single photograph should be taken showing all relevant detail and the relationships between things. Several photographs should also be taken from various angles to ensure all detail is captured.

Figure 9-5. Overhead and aerial photographs provide good detail, outlining roadway curves and markings.

Figure 9-6. When taking photographs, the camera must be held in a position that will not cause distortion of the roadway grade. In this example, the vehicle is parked on a steep incline although the picture depicts the roadway as being fairly level.

Figure 9-7. A picture should depict the scene as the driver or witness would have seen it. This is particularly true when recording the various series of events.

as to show the measurements of the tire tread and pattern, both sideways and longitudinal. This will allow exact measurements to be established later in relating the tire mark to suspect tires or to reconstruct the tire tread pattern to scale. However, whenever it is intended to use any form of marking or measuring device, always photograph the evidence first without them in the event a court of law might take exception to their presence in a picture.

Chapter 10

FAILURE TO REMAIN AT SCENE OF ACCIDENT

10.001   A hit-and-run accident is the failure by a *driver* to comply with any legal requirement regarding stopping, giving aid, and revealing identity following a *motor-vehicle traffic accident* in which he is involved.[1]

10.002   Use the same accident investigation procedures in a hit-and-run accident as in any other motor vehicle accident except enlarge the investigation to include locating a driver and vehicle involved.

10.003   Make immediate enquiries to locate *all* drivers involved in an accident. Determine whether a missing driver left the scene on foot or by vehicle. The missing driver may have been taken away for medical treatment by a passing motorist. When reasonably satisfied that a driver has illegally failed to remain at the scene of an accident, take special steps involving certain procedures to locate the driver and vehicle involved.

10.004   Notify the dispatch office that the accident involves a hit-and-run driver. Advise all patrol units, both locally and those of surrounding departments, providing as much descriptive detail of the driver and vehicle as possible. The longer the delay in providing this information the greater the offender's ability to establish an alibi, hide, destroy or repair his vehicle, or otherwise eliminate any evidence on his vehicle that might relate it to the accident. The following information should be included, when known.

Vehicle

   a. License plate number including issuing jurisdiction, e.g., state or province.
   b. Make, year, model, type and color of vehicle.
   c. Location and extent of damage to body, windshield or other part.
   d. Direction of travel.
   e. Other detail that will help in identifying the vehicle, e.g.,
      • grille features
      • burned out or broken headlights, tail-lights, etc.

- hood, fender, tail-pipe ornaments
- type and location of mirrors
- location and type of radio aerial
- description of tires, e.g., type of tread, white or blackwalls
- clean or dirty body
- new or faded paint job
- windshield and window stickers
- noise level of muffler
- noisy body parts, e.g., loose box, fender, tail-pipe, muffler, etc.

Driver and Passengers

a. Sex and age
b. Clothing, color, etc.
c. Complexion
d. Length and color of hair
e. Moustache
f. Sideburns
g. Eyeglasses
h. Stature, e.g., heavy set or slim, including seated height in vehicle.
i. The total number of passengers including seating positions of persons with identifiable features.

10.005 There are many reasons why a driver will flee the scene when involved in an accident with another vehicle or a pedestrian. Some of these are:

a. Driving while under the influence of alcohol or a drug.
b. Driving without a driver's license.
c. Driving without insurance coverage.
d. Married person accompanied by other than his or her spouse.
e. Having stolen goods in vehicle.
f. Fleeing another, previous accident.
g. Fleeing scene of criminal offense, e.g., armed robbery.
h. Driver "wanted" for a crime.
i. Panic struck. When a suspect driver is located and the only reason he has to offer for leaving the scene is that he was panic struck, his background, associates and activities just prior to the accident should be investigated.[2]
j. Being injured, e.g., suffering from concussion, and leaving scene

without criminal or civil intent, or leaving scene to obtain medical assistance.

10.006 When the hit-and-run driver and vehicle's identity is not established quickly, obtain all necessary assistance. The functions and duties of the various units and personnel assigned to an assistance role should be determined in advance of the need. Ensure responsibilities of each are well understood by everyone involved and efforts are properly coordinated.

10.007 Commence an on-scene investigation as soon as possible. Any delay may result in short-lived evidence and other valuable evidence being lost or destroyed. If a minute examination of the scene is required, it is advisable to cordon off the area to prevent damage to or loss of evidence. In complicated cases, it may be necessary to turn the investigation over to a special hit-and-run investigation unit.

10.008 Note and collect evidence at the scene that might be matched up to a suspect vehicle. This evidence includes:
   a. Broken glass from windows, windshield, headlights and other lights and mirrors.
   b. Broken body parts or items that might have fallen off of or have been thrown from the vehicle during collision, e.g.,
      (i) headlight parts, such as headlight rim.
      (ii) hub-caps, door handles; chrome pieces from the grille, fenders or side panels; bumper or bumper guards, tail-pipe extension, etc.
      (iii) paint chips or scrapings.
      (iv) portions of load.
      (v) soil or other debris that was knocked off or fell from vehicle, e.g., dirt from underside of fenders.
      (vi) tire prints.
      (vii) fluids, such as radiator fluid or oil.

10.009 If there is an indication that a driver or passenger was injured, check doctors' offices, hospitals and first-aid posts.

10.010 Record the time a vehicle theft is reported. If the report is received before a hit-and-run accident is established to have occurred, the thief could have been the driver. If the report is received sometime after a hit-and-run accident occurred, consider the possibility that the owner or someone known by him to have been the driver might have

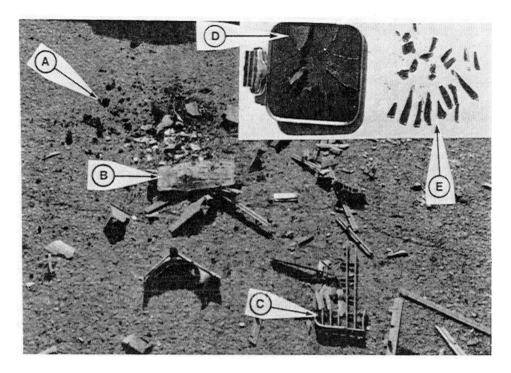

Figure 10-1. An example of vehicle parts found at an accident scene that can be matched to a hit-and-run vehicle. Note fender dirt (*A*), license-plate (*B*), grille part (*C*), and broken mirror (which may also be found on vehicle) (*D*) with matching glass fragments (*E*).

been driving at the time of the accident and the stolen car report was intended to mislead the investigation. Similarly, a vehicle that is reported to have been destroyed by fire, runaway over a cliff or embankment, etc., should be examined for evidence that might relate it to a hit-and-run accident.

10.011   When a report is received involving a parked vehicle, check the motor, tires and exhaust system for warmth. Also check the immediate vicinity for debris that would indicate that an accident did or did not in fact occur at that location. The driver may have been involved in an accident previously and driven the vehicle to that parked location in an attempt to cover up his involvement elsewhere.

10.012   Accept information from a willing bystander with some caution. A hit-and-run driver or one of his passengers, or some conspirator, may return to the scene and provide information with intent to mislead the investigation. Additionally, some people will attempt to be helpful, but

Figure 10-2. When a pedestrian is struck, parts of clothing (*A*) may adhere to or remain with the vehicle. The part of a vehicle that strikes a pedestrian may show damage (*B*) or other evidence of contact such as blood, flesh, etc.

because of their limited knowledge or information, they will manufacture certain details in order to make their own conclusions or opinions more plausible.

10.013   Examine and record the exact place and type of damage suffered by the victim's vehicle or by a pedestrian, etc., in a hit-and-run accident. When the victim is a person who is killed, it may be necessary to have hair samples taken before burial in order to match such samples against hair that might be found on a suspect vehicle at a later time. When a pedestrian is struck, record and, if possible, photograph the location of the injury so that the height of that portion of the vehicle that struck the pedestrian can be properly related.

10.014   Hold a victim's clothing as exhibits. Clothing patterns may be matched to pattern imprints left on a vehicle, and there may be paint samples embedded in the fabric itself.

10.015   Obtain samples of soil, roadway surface and/or debris left by the offending vehicle, such as dirt, from the accident scene. Particles from the roadway surface, e.g., fine gravel, oiled dirt or soft asphalt material, might have become lodged in tire treads, on the underside of the fenders or some other portion of the vehicle's body or frame. Debris left by the vehicle can often be matched to material found on a suspect vehicle. Also, certain types of dirt, e.g., red clay, can be related to individual sections of countryside, which in turn could give a location where the vehicle was commonly driven.

10.016   Collisions often cause the release of radiator fluid or oil from the motor or transmission. It is often possible to make an assumption as to how far a vehicle will be able to travel based on the amount of fluid loss. Patrols can then concentrate their efforts within a certain radius of the collision point. Fluid loss trails also allow for the direction of travel and vehicle movements to be traced.

10.017   The driver or a passenger may throw items out of their vehicle after an accident, e.g., beer bottles, stolen property, etc. These items may be found either on or off the highway and may have fingerprints on them, which might lead to the hit-and-run driver. Additionally, fingerprints may be left at the scene in instances where a driver stops to examine a victim or vehicle and touches the vehicle or some other item.

10.108   Vehicle parts may break loose or fall off at the time of collision and be vaulted or thrown a considerable distance in the direction the vehicle was travelling. These items may be found off the roadway as well as on the roadway.

10.019   Other items left at the scene by the offending vehicle or driver may be such things as envelopes, letters, business cards, etc., which may have the business or residence address of the owner, driver or passenger. Any such item found should be treated as valuable evidence.

10.020   The driver of a hit-and-run vehicle would have been travelling in the on-scene area for some reason. He may have been travelling to or from work. If the accident occurred in the late evening or early morning hours particularly, he may have been attending a house party or other function in the neighborhood. Attempt to relate the locale where the accident occurred to what the driver might have been doing in that area. The investigation should include going back through the pre-scene and pre-trip series of events in an attempt to determine where the driver might have been. Residents in the area where a house party was held, workers at a plant, the owner of a liquor outlet, etc., will often recognize the description of a vehicle and be able to describe its owner or driver.

10.021   Obtain the license plate number if possible. License plates show the state or province where they were issued. The series of letters or numerals also often indicate a particular city, town or county where they were issued. When the issuing jurisdiction is determined, patrol units should pay particular attention to traffic routes leading to those areas. If all numbers or letters comprising the license-plate identification are not available, any partial plate identification will be of value in eliminating other vehicles that would otherwise fit the description of the hit-and-run vehicle. Bear in mind that the driver may switch license-plates on his vehicle immediately after an accident occurs.

10.022   Examine a suspect vehicle for various types of evidence that might relate to or be matched up to evidence gathered at the accident scene. If the vehicle is located soon after the accident occurred, check the motor, radiator, exhaust system, brake drums and tires for warmth, which would indicate recent travel. If the vehicle is located some time after the accident occurred, examine it for any indication of recent repairs to the body and any repairs or replacement regarding other parts such as grille, lights, mirrors, hub-caps, bumpers, bumper guards, ornaments, etc., at the same time bearing in mind the type of damage suffered by the victim's vehicle, pedestrian or other object at the time of collision.

10.023   Examine the undercarriage, grille, all protruding parts (e.g., mirrors, fender and hood ornaments) and damaged areas for blood, hair, clothing fabrics, paint chips or scrapings, tire marks and other similar evidence that might be matched to the object struck.

10.024   A hit-and-run driver may put different tires on his vehicle in order to avoid detection when tire prints might be used as evidence. For example, he may replace new tires with old, worn tires; worn tires with new tires, and mix the tread patterns.

10.025   Do not confine the investigation to the on-scene area. Extend it to the pre-scene and post-scene areas as well. Unsafe or erratic driving behaviour by the hit-and-run driver may have been seen some distance before the actual collision area by other motorists, garagemen, store owners, etc. Similarly, erratic driving or the damaged vehicle might have been seen by other motorists or individuals after it left the accident scene. If the accident occurred during darkness, a headlight or other light may have been broken and the driver may have stopped at a garage or service station to have it replaced, or to have other repairs made to the vehicle.

10.026 Request the assistance of the news media in locating the suspect vehicle and driver. Radio news broadcasts, for example, normally cover a great area giving considerable coverage to the description of a suspect vehicle. Considerable help can be expected from the motoring public when such broadcasts are made. Additionally, broadcasts over civilian band radio systems to truck operators, car clubs, etc., and taxi operators can be of considerable assistance in disseminating information regarding a hit-and-run driver and vehicle.

10.027 Check surrounding areas where the vehicle might have been abandoned, hidden or otherwise removed from immediate sight. These areas should include garages, auto body repair shops, parking lots, and places where the vehicle could be placed among other vehicles and not be readily seen.

10.028 Visit the accident scene on subsequent days, particularly the same day of following weeks. Note the descriptions of vehicles travelling in the same direction as the hit-and-run vehicle was travelling. Newly painted vehicles, damaged or apparently recently repaired vehicles should be investigated.

10.029 Garages, vehicle dealers and vehicle supply outlets are often able to identify the make and model of a vehicle from a broken part left at the scene. These businesses should also be requested to assist in an investigation by advising the police if a replacement part is ordered or purchased. Similarly, auto body repair shops should be advised to contact the police should a vehicle answering the description of the hit-and-run vehicle come to their attention.

REFERENCES

1. Baker, J. Stannard: *Traffic Accident Investigation Manual.* Traffic Institute, Northwestern University, Evanston, Illinois, 1975, p. 316.
2. Rivers, R.W.: *Traffic Accident Investigator's Handbook.* Charles C Thomas, Springfield, Illinois, 1980, p. 259–260.

Chapter 11

FIELD SKETCHES, MAPS AND DIAGRAMS

11.001   Accurate measurements must be taken at the scene in order to give court testimony, prepare a scale diagram or to reconstruct an accident. Sufficient measurements must also be taken. Generally, the seriousness of an accident will dictate the extent to which measurements should be taken. All fatal and serious personal injury accidents should, however, be thoroughly investigated including comprehensive field measurements.

11.002   The on-scene investigator should immediately take measurements of things that will be quickly removed, lost or destroyed. These include oil spills, faint skid marks, etc. When an object must be moved or there is an indication that the evidence will be lost or destroyed because of such things as passing traffic, the investigator should mark its location on the roadway with crayon or other means so that its original position may be measured later.

FIELD SKETCH

11.003   Measurements should be recorded on a field sketch. A *field sketch* is a freehand map of the scene or site of an accident, showing certain features of the accident or road configuration, usually for the purpose of recording measurements.[1] The on-scene investigator should immediately complete a *preliminary field sketch* showing the positions and measurements of short-lived evidence and things that must be immediately moved or removed. A field sketch should be prepared by first showing an outline of the roadways and then filling in all things in their relative position to each other together with adequate measurements. The symbols shown in Figure 11-1 may be used in preparing a field sketch and scale diagram (*See* Fig. 11-2).

11.004   A field sketch is part of an investigator's field notes, recording many of his observations. Once completed, the sketch should not be rewritten for sake of neatness, as this could affect the admissibility in

126

BODY	ROADWAY REFLECTOR BUTTONS	FENCES (Various)	STREAM
PEDESTRIAN	MANHOLE COVER	PROPERTY LINE	WATER
PASSENGER CAR	SKIDMARK		OBSTRUCTION OR HAZARD
TRUCK TRACTOR	TIREPRINT	ROADWAY LANE MARKINGS	RAILWAY TRACKS
TRUCK. BUS. TRAILER	YAW OR SIDESLIP MARK	GROOVE OR FURROW	ROADWAY LANE DIVIDER
MOTORCYCLE	SCRUB OR SCUFF MARK	SCRATCHES OR SCRAPE MARKS	COMPASS DIRECTION
BICYCLE	CURB	CHIPS AND GOUGES	SIGHT LINE
DIRECTION OF THRUST	ROADWAY EDGE	PUDDLE, RUNOFF AND TRAILS FLUID	CAMERA ANGLE
POSITION OF DAMAGE	SHOULDER EDGE	DEBRIS	DIRECTION OF SUN
TRAFFIC SIGNAL LIGHTS	DITCH	UTILITY POLE	CLOUD OR FOG
SIGNS (Specify)	EMBANKMENT	STREEP LAMP	RAIN: OR SNOW WITH DIRECTION
RAILWAY COSSING	ABUTMENT	TREE	GRADE OR SUPERELEVATION +0.04
ROADWAY MUSHROOM BUTTONS	GUARD RAIL	SHRUBBERY	SCALE 0 10 20

Figure 11-1. Symbols are useful in preparing field sketches, diagrams and maps.

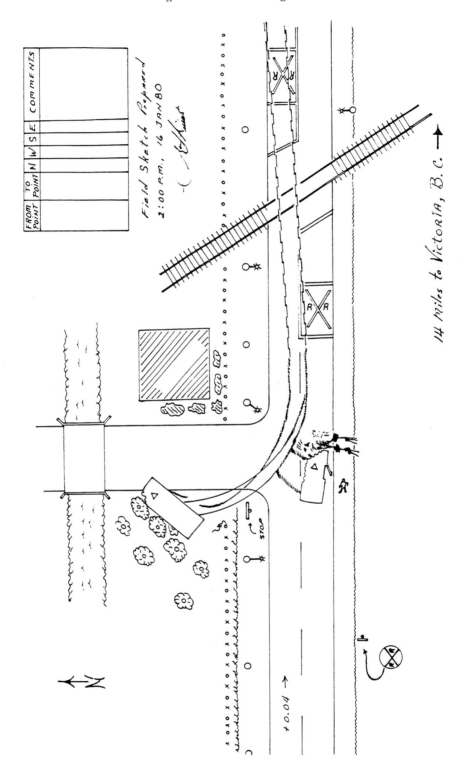

Figure 11-2. Method of using symbols in a field sketch.

Figure 11-3. Tangible reference points such as those found on overpass and bridge structures, utility poles, etc., may be used to locate accident locations.

court of the measurements taken and other information recorded on the sketch. If a mistake is made, do not erase the mistake, but cross it out and write in and initial the correction.[2]

MEASURING THE SCENE

11.005 When measuring up an accident scene, certain procedures should be followed to ensure accuracy.

a. Establish one or more permanent reference points (tangible RP), e.g., tree, fire hydrant, crack in curbing, manhole cover, etc., from which to take measurements. Other reference points may be marked on the roadway with a crayon (intangible RP) in order to relate all measurements and objects. All intangible RPs should, however, be measured and related to the tangible RPs being used.

b. For reasons of safety, measurements should be taken along the edge of the roadway whenever possible. Use curb lines and roadway edges as baselines. At intersections where curbs are rounded, extension lines may be marked on the pavement and the point where they intersect then becomes an intangible RP from which measurements may be taken. (*See* Fig. 11-6.)

c. Have an assistant hold the "zero" end of a measuring tape.

d. Take measurements to the closest inch or even centimeter.

e. The investigator who reads the measuring device must also be the one who records measurements taken.

f. The use of the apostrophe (') or quote mark (") to indicate feet and inches can be mistaken for the numbers 1 and 11. Therefore, feet and inches should be recorded as in the following examples:
Record ten feet and two inches as 10^2
Record twelve feet as 12^0
Record sixteen inches as *16*

g. Some measuring devices are marked in feet and tenths of a foot. When recording these measurements, use the decimal point to set out the tenths of a foot in the following manner:
Record seven feet as 7.0
Record seven and five-tenths feet as 7.5

h. When using the metric system of measurement, indicate whether the measurements are in centimeters (cm), meters (m) or kilometers (km).
Record 8.24 centimeters as 8.24 cm
Record 8.24 meters as 8.24 m
Record 8.24 kilometers as 8.24 km
Because most accident scene measurements will be taken in meters or parts of a meter, it is acceptable to show all measurements in meters or parts of a meter without being followed by the "m" designation provided that any other measurement such as centimeters also taken at the scene or otherwise recorded in the investigation is properly designated.[3]

i. When measurements are longer than the tape measure being used, place a crayon mark on the roadway including the number of feet (meters) at the end of the tape. Have the assistant who is holding the "zero" end of the tape come to this mark and then continue with additional measurements.

j. For great distances, e.g., 1000 feet (300 meters), determine the average length of roadway broken center lines and distances that separate them, or the average distance between utility poles along the highway. By multiplying their numbers over the distance being measured, that distance may be *estimated.*

k. The investigator should choose the scale he wishes to use for drawing a scale diagram. For example, he may wish to choose an inch or any part thereof to represent one foot, or a millimeter or one centimeter to represent one meter or a greater number of meters.

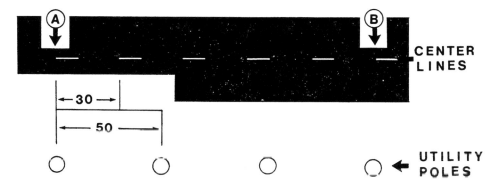

Figure 11-4. The average lengths of broken center lines and the distances that separate them or the distances between utility poles may be measured and multiplied by their number to obtain the measurement required. Example: 5 × 30 = 150; 3 × 50 = 150.

GRADE

11.006 *Grade* is the change in elevation in unit distance in a specified direction along the center line of a *roadway* or the path of a vehicle, the difference in level of two points divided by the level distance between the points. Grade is designated in feet per foot (meters per meter) of rise or fall per foot (meter) of level distance or in rise or fall as a percent of the level distance. Grade is positive (+) if the surface rises in the specified direction and negative (−) if it falls in that direction.[4]

11.007 *Superelevation* (bank) is the grade *across* the roadway at right angles to the center line from the inside to the outside edge on a curve.[5]

11.008 Grade and superelevation should be shown on a field sketch, indicating the percent grade, whether it is positive or negative, and its direction by using an arrow (*See* Fig. 11-2).

United States	*S.I.*
$e = \dfrac{r}{L} \times \dfrac{100}{1}$	$e = \dfrac{r}{L} \times \dfrac{100}{1}$

where e = percentage grade ($\pm$)
  r = rise or falla
  L = length or distance

$$e = \frac{12}{120} \times \frac{100}{1}$$ $$e = \frac{30}{300} \times \frac{100}{1}$$

$$e = 10\%$$ $$e = 10\%$$

11.009   A grade may be measured by using a *clinometer,* which is an instrument for determining angular inclination of such things as slopes. Another method of measuring grade is to use a carpenter's level in the manner outlined in Fig. 11-5. In this example, if the length (L) of the board were 120 in. (300 cm) and the rise or fall (r) was 12 in. (30 cm), the percentage grade (e) could be calculated by using Formula 11-1:

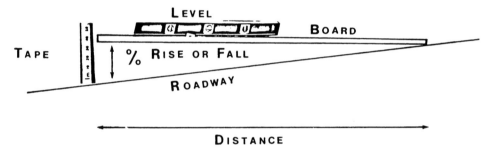

Figure 11-5. A method of measuring the grade or superelevation of a roadway using a carpenter's level. (See also Fig. 12-5.)

METHODS OF MEASURING

11.010   There are two basic methods of measuring traffic accident scenes.
  1. *Triangulation method.* Triangulation is a method of locating a spot in an area by measurements from two or more reference points, the locations of which are identified for future reference.[6]
  To fix the position of a small object or item, e.g., body, blood spot, etc., measure to its center from at least two reference points. Larger objects should have at least two points fixed by triangulation measured from at least two reference points. Long, thin triangles should be avoided because they are very difficult to use in preparing a scale diagram or repositioning things at the location.

2. *Coordinate method.* Coordinates are distances measured at right angles from a baseline to an object or point.[7] A reasonably straight roadway edge will usually suffice as a baseline. The points along a baseline from which coordinate measurements are made must be measured and related to a permanent or tangible reference point.

11.011   The investigator will find that under some circumstances it is desirable to use both the triangulation and coordinate methods in measuring an accident scene. This is particularly true in measuring the location of skid marks and other evidence that must be related to in giving testimony in court cases.

MEASURING CURVES AND INTERSECTIONS

11.012   A curve is a part of a circle or an arc. To determine the size or degree of a circle, it is necessary to first calculate the circle's radius. The radius (R) of a curvey may be calculated by using Formula 11-2:

United States

$$R = \frac{C^2}{8M} + \frac{M}{2}$$

S.I.

$$R = \frac{C^2}{8M} + \frac{M}{2}$$

Where R = Radius
$\quad\quad C$ = Chord
$\quad\quad M$ = Middle ordinate

To measure a curve (*See* Fig. 11-11), find points *a* and *b*, which are just before the places where the curve straightens out. The distance between *a* and *b* is the *Chord, C.* Divide the Chord in half for point *c*. Measure from *c* at a right angle to the arc to find point *d*. The distance from *c* to *d* is the Middle Ordinate, *M*.

Example 1
In figure 11-11: C = 50 ft. (15.24 m) and M = 6 ft. (1.83 m).
Applying Formula 11-2,

$$R = \frac{50^2}{8 \times 6} + \frac{6}{2}$$

$$R = \frac{2500}{48} + \frac{6}{2}$$

$$R = 52 + 3$$

$$R = 55 \text{ feet}$$

$$R = \frac{15.24^2}{8 \times 1.83} + \frac{1.83}{2}$$

$$R = \frac{232.26}{14.64} + \frac{1.83}{2}$$

$$R = 15.86 + .92$$

$$R = 16.78 \text{ meters}$$

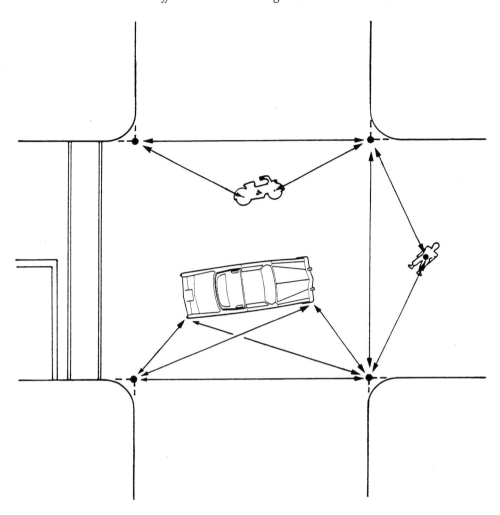

Figure 11-6. Method of using triangulation to locate vehicles, bodies or other objects. In this example, intangible reference points, namely: curb extensions, are used.

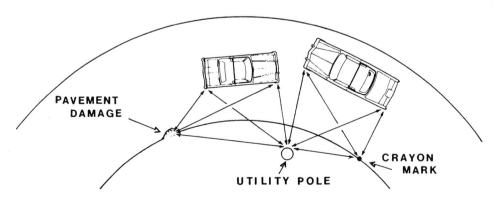

Figure 11-7. Method of using triangulation to locate vehicles on a curve. In this example, both tangible and intangible reference points are used.

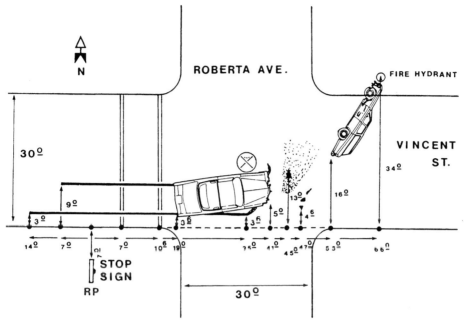

Figure 11-8. Method of using coordinates to locate things on a roadway. In this example, measurements are recorded on the sketch or diagram.

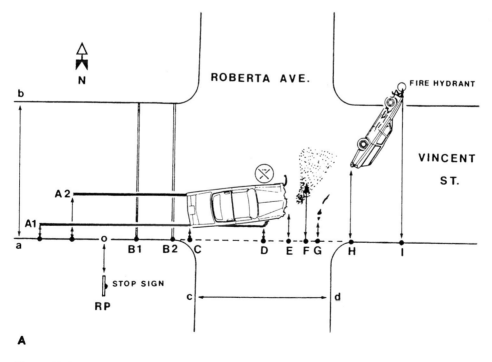

A

Figure 11-9 A. Method of recording field measurements relating a sketch (*A*) to a table (*B*).

FROM POINT	TO POINT	N	W	S	E	COMMENTS
O	A-1	3°	14°			
O	A-2	9°	7°			
O	B-1				7°	Lead side of x-walk
O	B-2				10⁶	
O	C	3⁶			19°	
O	D	3⁶			35°	end of skidmark and beginning of scrubmark
O	E	5°			41°	Right front of vehicle
O	F	13°			45°	Center of debris
O	G	4⁶			47°	Gouges in roadway
O	H	16°			55°	
O	I	34°			66°	Front of vehicle against fire hydrant
c	d					Roadway width of Roberta Ave. = 30°
a	b					Vincent St. = 30ᵉ

B

Figure 11-9 B.

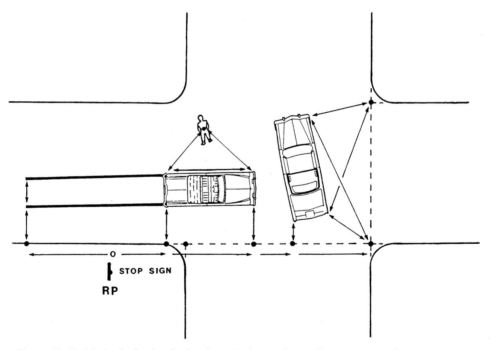

Figure 11-10. Method of using both triangulation and coordinates to record measurements.

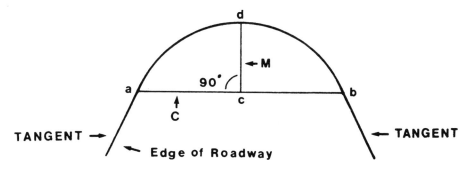

Figure 11-11. Parts of a curve. *a* to *b* represents the chord, *C. c* to *d* represents the middle ordinate, *M*. Where the curve straightens out are tangents. Source: *Traffic Accident Investigators' Handbook* by Rivers. Courtesy Charles C Thomas, Publisher, Springfield, Illinois.

Figure 11-12. Method of measuring various radii of a large curve.

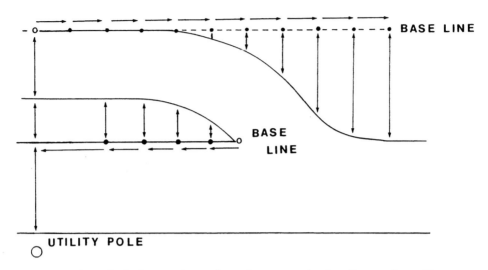

Figure 11-13. Method of measuring an irregular curve using baselines and coordinates.

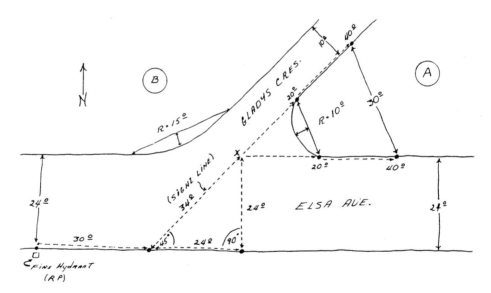

Figure 11-14 A. Field sketch.

Figure 11-14 B. Method of making field measurements of a curve.

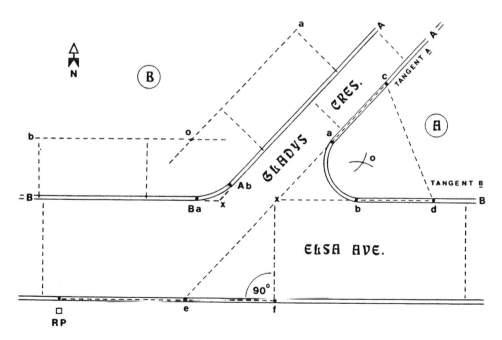

Figure 11-14 C. Scale diagram.

Once the radius of one point of a curve is known, the radius of another point may be indirectly calculated by adding or subtracting its distance from the known radius.

Example 2

In Figure 11-12, the roadway edge (*C*) radius is known to be 55 ft. (16.78 m). The radius of the center line would be 55 + 12 or 67 feet (16.78 + 3.66 or 20.44 meters)

11.013   A curve on an acute angle such as that at Corner *A* of the field sketch (Fig. 11-14A) may be drawn to scale in the following manner (*See* Fig. 11-14C):

   a. Draw in road edges as lines *A* and *B* at the correct angle so that they meet at an apex, point *x*.
   b. From point *x*, mark in points *a* and *b* along lines *A* and *B* where the curve begins. In the case of corner *A*, this distance is 20 feet. Beyond these points, the edges are straight and are considered tangents (Tan) of the curve.
   c. Set the compass at 10 feet (the radius of the curve) at the scale being used.
   d. Place the compass pinpoint at points *a* and *b* and scribe arcs that bisect each other at point *o*.
   e. Place the compass pinpoint at point *o* and scribe an arc from *a* to *b*. This completes the curve to scale.

11.014   When a street intersects another street at an angle other than 90 degrees, special field measurements are required in order to plot the intersection on a scale diagram. Using the intersection at corner *A* in the field sketch Figure 11-14A for example, field measurements and the field sketch should include the following (*See* Fig. 11-14C):

   a. Measure back from the apex *x* for a convenient distance to *c* and *d*.
   b. Measure the distance from *c* to *d*. This completes the triangle and fixes the angle of the intersecting street.
   c. Sight along tangent *A* to the curb line of Elsa Avenue to establish point *e*. Measure along the edge of Elsa Avenue from point *e* to establish point *f* that, when measured to point *x* at an angle of 90 degrees, will complete a triangle.
   d. Measure from the reference point (*RP*) along Elsa Avenue to point *e*. This measurement fixes the position of Gladys Crescent at its intersection with Elsa Avenue.

11.015   To plot the angle at which Gladys Crescent intersects Elsa Avenue on a scale diagram (Fig. 11-14C) using the measurements from the field sketch (Fig. 11-14A):

a. Measure the distance from the fire hydrant (*RP*) to point *e*, mark it and then measure to point *f*. Measure from point *f* at 90 degrees to point *x*. Mark a line from *x* to *e* to complete a triangle. This establishes *x* in relation to the reference point (*RP*).

b. The angle of tangent *B* to point *x* is already known, being the north edge of Elsa Avenue.

c. From point *e*, follow along the hypotenuse of the triangle to *x* and draw a continuing line 20 feet further to *a* and 40 feet to *c*, forming tangent *A*.

d. Similarly, from point *x* draw a line to *b* and *d* along tangent *B*.

e. As a check of the work, measure the distance from *c* to *d*, which should be as shown on the field sketch.

11.016   When the radius of a curve is known, the curve may be placed on a scale diagram. In corners *A* and *B* of the field sketch (Fig. 11-15A), for example, the radii are 10 feet. These curves may be plotted on a scale diagram (*See* Fig. 11-15C) in the following manner.[8]

a. Draw in street edges. Show the streets where the curve is to be completed as intersecting at the correct angle (Point *x*).

b. Draw construction lines *a* and *b* 10 feet (the length of the radius)

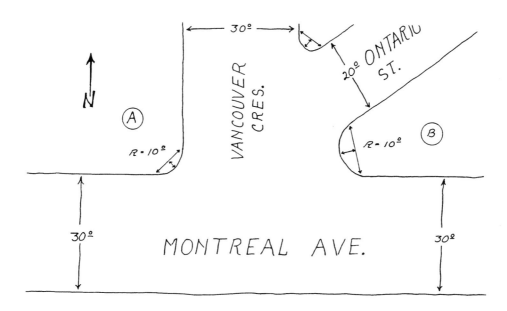

Figure 11-15 A. Field sketch.

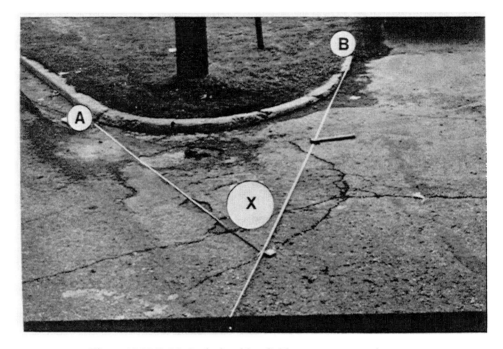

Figure 11-15 B. Method of making field measurements of a curve.

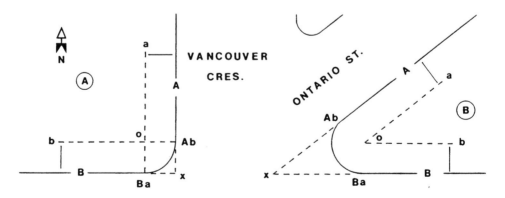

Figure 11-15 C. Scale diagram.

inside and parallel to the curb lines *A* and *B*. Where lines *a* and *b* intersect each other, mark point *o*.

   c. Set compass at 10 feet at the scale being used. Place compass pinpoint at *o* and scribe an arc from *Ab* to *Ba* (where the curve starts) to complete the curve.

This same procedure may be followed to reconstruct the curve in corner *B* of the field sketch Figure 11-14A (*See also* Fig. 11-14C).

11.017 An offset, Ryan Street in the field sketch (Fig. 11-16A) for example, may be plotted on a scale diagram in the following manner (*See* Fig. 11-16B):

   a. Draw in Deanne Avenue and Lawrence Street to scale.

   b. Measure from the curb extension lines (*RP*) at Lawrence Street eastward to point *a*, which is in direct line with the west edge of Ryan Street.

   c. Draw in line *b* at 90 degrees from point *a*, northward to desired length to form the west edge of Ryan Street.

   d. Plot the width of Ryan Street, *c* to *d*, and draw another line parallel to line *b* to form the east edge of Ryan Street.

   e. Complete the edges of Ryan Street with permanent lines. Construct all corners to scale and erase unnecessary construction lines.

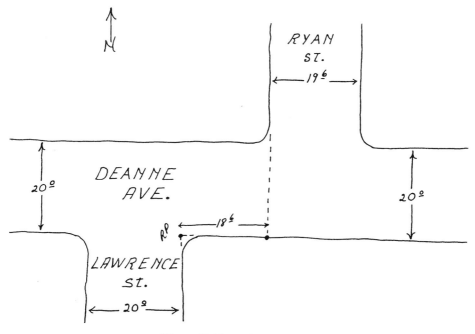

Figure 11-16 A. Field sketch.

MEASURING INTO LAKES AND RIVERS

11.018   The position of a vehicle in a river or lake, or in some other location that makes it difficult to measure, may be measured indirectly by using congruent triangles (*See* Fig. 11-17).

   a. Lay a baseline (*BD*) at a convenient length. The end of the baseline (*B*) must be at a right angle (90 degrees) to the point of the vehicle being measured, namely, point *A*.

   b. Find the midpoint of the baseline and mark it *C. B* to *C* and *C* to *D* will be equal in length.

   c. From *D*, proceed at an angle of 90 degrees (south in this example) to a point where *C* may be sighted in direct line with point *A*. Mark this point *E*.

   d. Measure the distance from point *D* to point *E*. This distance will be equal to the distance the vehicle is in the water because in congruent triangles, sides and angles are equal.

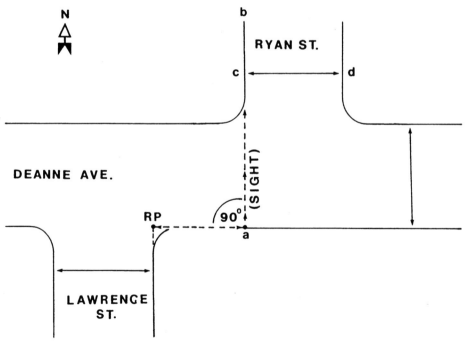

Figure 11-16 B. Scale diagram.

Figure 11-17.

REFERENCES

1. Baker, J. Stannard: *Traffic Accident Investigation Manual.* Traffic Institute, Northwestern University, Evanston, Illinois, 1975, p. 316.
2. Rivers, R.W.: *Traffic Accident Investigator's Handbook.* Charles C Thomas, Springfield, Illinois, 1980, p. 287.
3. Rivers, R.W.: *Traffic Accident Investigator's Handbook.* Charles C Thomas, Springfield, Illinois, 1980, p. 274.
4. Baker, J. Stannard: *Traffic Accident Investigation Manual.* Traffic Institute, Northwestern University, Evanston, Illinois, 1975, pp. 316–317.
5. Baker, J. Stannard: *Traffic Accident Investigation Manual.* Traffic Institute, Northwestern University, Evanston, Illinois, 1971, p. 360.
6. Baker, J. Stannard: *Traffic Accident Investigation Manual.* Traffic Institute, Northwestern University, Evanston, Illinois, 1975, p. 321.
7. Rivers, R.W.: *Traffic Accident Investigator's Handbook.* Charles C Thomas, Springfield, Illinois, 1980, p. 294.
8. Rivers, R.W.: *Traffic Accident Investigator's Handbook.* Charles C Thomas, Springfield, Illinois, 1980, p. 299.

Chapter 12

SPEED ESTIMATES

INTRODUCTION TO SPEED ESTIMATES

12.001 *Speed* may be a contributing factor in most traffic accidents. Therefore, one of the most important aspects of traffic accident investigation or reconstruction is to establish a vehicle's estimated speed at the time of or immediately before collision.

12.002 In this manual, except when the context provides otherwise, a reference to *speed* means a measurement in miles per hour (kilometers per hour) and is designated by upper case letter **S**. A reference to velocity means a measurement in feet per second (meters per second), and is designated by lower case letter **v**.

12.003 Speed estimates may be made by one or a combination of the following:
  a. Skid marks
  b. Yaw marks
  c. Vehicle damage
  d. Witness statement

12.004 The most commonly used method of establishing a vehicle's speed is calculating minimum speed based on skid marks. To use skid marks for this purpose, the following must be known:
  a. Skid distance (slide to stop)
  b. Coefficient of friction (μ) or drag factor (f)
  c. Roadway grade or superelevation
  d. The number of wheels that were braking
  e. Vehicle did not strike a substantial object before skidding to a stop
  f. Vehicle was not towing a trailer unless the trailer was equipped with brakes that were applied at approximately the same time as the towing vehicle brakes

PROFESSIONAL RECONSTRUCTIONIST

12.005   Professional traffic accident reconstructionists are often able to estimate vehicle speeds from the amount of body damage and distortion, primarily from the extent of penetration of one vehicle by another. When it is necessary to calculate speed in this manner, it is essential that photographs and measurements be taken adequate to meet the requirements of such calculations.

SKID MARK MEASUREMENTS

12.006   In measuring the length of skid marks for speed calculation purposes, certain determinations must be made and certain procedures followed.

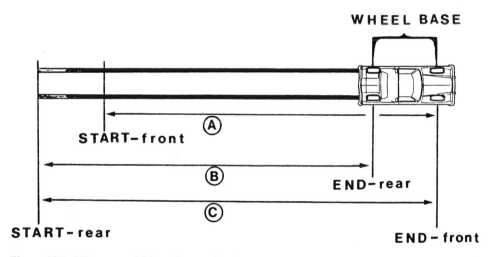

Figure 12-1. When rear skid marks overlap front skid marks, i.e., rear tires skid directly over front tire skid marks, subtract the wheel base distance from the average length of both skid marks or from the distance from the start to the end of skid. In this example, *C* represents the total length of the overlapping skid mark. *A* and *B* are the distances the vehicle actually skidded. (Source: *Traffic Accident Investigators' Handbook* by Rivers. Courtesy Charles C Thomas, Publisher, Springfield, Illinois.)

   a. The *beginning* and the *end* of each skid mark must be determined. An *impending skid mark* should be included in an overall skid mark length (*See* paragraph 7.031 *and* Fig. 7-29).
   b. *Measurements* should be taken to at least the closest six inches (15 cm) in general skid mark measurements. An investigator should

also adopt a proper, easily understood format for recording skid mark lengths (*See* Figs. 11-8 and 11-9).

c. *Markers* should be used to show specific locations, e.g., beginning of impending skid mark, etc., for photographic purposes. When markers are used, photographs should also be taken without markers to avoid admissibility arguments in court.

d. The *longest skid mark* may be used as the skid distance when it is known that all wheels locked at about the same time. For record purposes, however, all skid mark lengths should be measured (*See* Figs. 12-1 and 12-2).

e. When wheels do not lock at the same time or when there is considerable variance in skid mark lengths, all skid mark lengths should be measured and the *average length* used as the skid distance.

f. In *overlapping skid marks,* the total length of the skid marks should be measured. The skid distance will be this length minus the length of the vehicle's wheel base (*See* Fig. 12-1).

g. *Skip skid marks* should be measured as one continuous skid mark from the beginning of the first skid mark to the end of the last skid mark for each wheel (*See* Fig. 7-34).

h. *Intermittent skid marks* should be measured separately and in the same manner as a single skid. Their sum should then be used as the total skid distance. It should be remembered that each skid mark may have an impending skid mark that should be included in the measurement. (*See* Fig. 7-33.)

i. A *curved skid mark* should be measured by letting the measuring device follow the path of the skid mark around the curve.

j. *Dual-wheel skid marks* are to be measured as a single skid mark. When one tire of a dual-wheel leaves a longer skid mark than the other, the longer mark should be used as the skid distance for that wheel (*See* Fig. 12-3).

k. When a skid mark traverses *different kinds of roadway surfaces,* the length of the skid mark on each surface should be measured separately. This is required because of the different *f* values involved in calculating speed in these particular situations.

COEFFICIENT OF FRICTION

12.007 *Coefficient of friction.* Coefficient of friction (designated by the Greek letter μ, pronounced **"mew"**) represents *the sliding resistance between*

Figure 12-2. Use the longest skid mark as the skid distance when all wheels lock up at approximately the same time. A conservative measurement of the skid distance may be made by averaging the distance of all skid marks.

Figure 12-3. Dual wheel skid marks. In this example, skid mark *A* is the same length as skid mark *B* because in the case of skid mark *B* the measurement is taken from the first indication of a skid to the last indication of a skid of that dual wheel unit. (Source: *Traffic Accident Investigators' Handbook* by Rivers. Courtesy Charles C Thomas, Publisher, Springfield, Illinois.)

two surfaces when one of the surfaces is level, i.e., without grade or slope, and the other slides over that surface in a continuous motion. An example of such resistance is the *friction, traction or adhesion* between a tire and a level highway surface when the tire is skidding on that surface. Coefficient of friction is measured as a ratio based of two forces: (1) the horizontal force (i.e., pull) parallel to the level surface that is required to keep the object in continuous motion in the direction of the force *divided* by (2) the normal or perpendicular force exerted by the object onto the surface over which it is sliding. *Coefficient of friction applies only if vehicles have all wheels locked up, thus providing 100% braking efficiency when sliding on a level surface* (See Fig. 12-4).

Formula 12-1

United States   S.I.

$$\mu = \frac{F}{W}$$

$$\mu = \frac{F}{W}$$

where μ = coefficient of friction
       F = horizontal force (pull) required to cause an object's continuous movement on a level surface
     W = normal or perpendicular force (or weight of object) pressing against the surface

DRAG FACTOR

12.008 *Drag factor.* Like coefficient of friction, drag factor (designated by the letter f) is a measurement of the friction, traction or adhesion between one surface sliding over another surface and is based on the force (pull) required to keep the sliding object in continuous motion in the direction of the force **divided** by the weight of the sliding object. Like coefficient of friction, drag factor is expressed as a decimal fraction. The decimal fraction here, however, is the ratio of the acceleration or deceleration of the sliding object to the acceleration of gravity (f = a/g). This equation is explained in greater detail under the skid mark and drag sled testing procedures that follow.

Formula 12-2

United States   S.I.

$$f = \frac{F}{W}$$

$$f = \frac{F}{W}$$

where f = drag factor
      F = horizontal force (pull) required to cause an object's object's continuous sliding movement on a surface
     W = normal or perpendicular force of object (or weight of object) pressing against the surface

Example

A fully-braked, four-wheel vehicle (one having 100% braking efficiency) was moved with its wheels locked up over a **level** roadway surface. The vehicle weighed 4,000 lbs (1814.36 kg). The force required to give it constant speed, was 2,000 lbs (907.18 kg). The drag factor (and the coefficient of friction) was:

$$f = \frac{2,000}{4,000}$$

$$f = .50$$

$$f = \frac{907.18}{1814.36}$$

$$f = .50$$

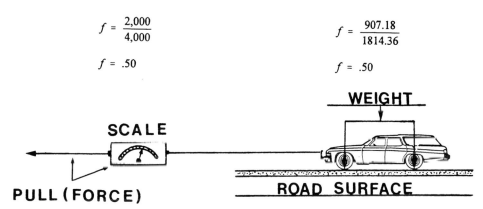

Figure 12-4. Illustration of drag factor or roadway coefficient of friction (Source: *Traffic Accident Investigators' Handbook* by rivers. Courtesy of Charles C Thomas, Publisher, Springfield, Illinois).

12.009 Coefficient of friction and drag factor sometimes turn out to have the same numerical value: μ, the measurement of the drag resistance between two objects, is equal to f, the measurement of the force required to overcome that resistance. Having two terms is useful in that one can then specifically indicate either of these aspects of the friction phenomenon. Also, as will be explained presently, there is only one condition under which the values are equal in a technical sense. (See para's. 12.007 and 12.011.)

12.010 In the case of *drag factor,* sliding need not be only on a level surface, but rather it can be also on a surface having a grade or slope. In addition to being used with vehicles having 100 percent braking efficiency, it can also be applied to a situation that involves vehicles having less than 100 percent braking efficiency on one or all wheels; commercial-type vehicles where all wheels do not lock up at the same time; vehicles where weight shift is considered a factor; friction generated by a tire sideslipping on a roadway surface in a turn or curve; friction generated between a tire and the roadway surface when the drive wheels are under acceleration; friction generated by a body, vehicle part or any other object moving or sliding over a roadway surface or any other surface.

12.011   In a technical sense, the only time coefficient of friction and drag factor values are equal is when a four wheel vehicle with all wheels locked up, thus providing 100% braking efficiency, skids on a **level** surface. However, the terms *coefficient of friction* and *drag factor,* as used in many traffic accident investigation textbooks, are considered synonymous (identical in meaning). For the purposes of this manual, the terms will be treated as synonymous, that is to say, as representing the stopping force expressed as a numerical value of slipperiness (written as a decimal fraction), and unless circumstances dictate otherwise, only the term *drag factor,* and designated with the letter *f,* will be used.

Coefficient of Friction and Drag Factor

General definition. The general definition of the terms *coefficient of friction* and *drag factor* is:

The sliding resistance, e.g., *friction, traction* or *adhesion* (stopping force) between two surfaces, written as a decimal fraction expressing a numerical value of slipperiness.

An example is a vehicle tire sliding or skidding over a roadway surface. See paragraphs 12.007 and 12.008 for definitive definitions of both terms.

12.012   Drag factor may be determined by:
  a. Conducting test skids.
  b. Pulling a tire and wheel, or other object, over the roadway surface.
  c. Using a drag sled.
  d. Referring to the **Coefficient of Friction (Drag Factor) Guide,** Table 12-1, following paragraph 12.040.

NOTE: UNDER NO CIRCUMSTANCES SHOULD TEST SKIDS, OR ANY OTHER TEST, BE MADE WHEN THERE IS A DANGER OF CAUSING AN ACCIDENT, INJURY OR DAMAGE. AS A GENERAL RULE, TEST SKIDS SHOULD NOT BE CARRIED OUT AT A SPEED GREATER THAN 35 MPH (56 KM/H). THE PREVAILING CONDITIONS WILL OFTEN DICTATE HOW THE DRAG FACTOR WILL BE DETERMINED. FOR EXAMPLE, TEST SKIDS USUALLY

WILL NOT BE CARRIED OUT ON ICY SURFACES, BUT A DRAG SLED MAY BE USED.

12.013–12.015 reserved.

GRADE OR SLOPE AND SUPERELEVATION

12.016 *Grade* or *slope* is the change in elevation in unit distance in a specified direction along the center line of a roadway or the path of a vehicle. Superelevation (bank) is the grade across the roadway at right angles to the center line from the inside to the outside edge on a curve. Grade and superelevation are expressed and used as a decimal fraction. For example, a 10 percent rise or fall is expressed as +0.10 or   0.10, a 4 percent rise or fall is expressed as +0.04 or −0.04, respectively. They are considered positive (+) if the surface rises in the specified direction and negative (−) if it falls in that direction. (See also para. 11.006 and Fig. 11-5.)

12.017 Grade and superelevation may be measured by using a clinometer, which is an instrument for determining the angular inclination of surfaces. Other methods of measuring grade involve the use of a traffic template, such as **IPTM's blueBlitz Traffic Template**® (see Fig. 12-5) or use a carpenter's level as illustrated in Figure 11-5. In the first of these, the grade can be read directly from the traffic template. In the second, the grade can be calculated as explained in paragraph 11.009.

2.018–2.020 reserved.

TEST SKIDS

12.021 When test skids are carried out to determine the drag factor, preferably the accident vehicle or similar vehicle should be used, and the conditions under which such tests are conducted must duplicate as closely as possible the conditions experienced at the time of the accident, to include the following:
   a. Type of roadway surface
   b. Direction of travel
   c. Vehicle load
   d. Roadway temperature
   e. Roadway surface conditions

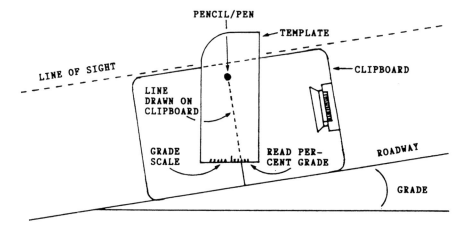

Figure 12-5. Template suspended from the round pencil/pen inserted through the hole in the clipboard and able to swing freely; roadway edge of the clipboard placed on the roadway; grade scale at the bottom of the template giving the percent grade reading where the line drawn on the clipboard crosses the grade scale. (Sources: R.W. Rivers *Traffic Accident Field Measurements and Scale Diagrams Manual,* Charles C Thomas, Publisher, Springfield, Illinois, 1983, pp 38 and 48; and R.W. Rivers, *blueBlitz Traffic Template Instruction Manual,* Institute of Police Technology and Management, University of North Florida, Jacksonville, Flordia, 1985, p. 11.)

12.022   Motorcycles, large buses and trucks present special problems. Test skids and speed estimates for these types of vehicles are generally beyond the scope of this manual. (See, however, para. 12.048 and its example.)

Speedometer Accuracy Test

12.023   When test skids are conducted, using other than the accident vehicle for the tests, it is important that the accuracy of the speedometer be known.

Formula 12-3

United States	*S.I.*
$S = \dfrac{3600}{t}$	$S = \dfrac{3600}{t}$

where S = actual speed
t = time in seconds to travel measured mile or kilometer at a constant (speedometer) speed

Example

It took a vehicle 62 seconds to travel a measured mile (kilometer). The speedometer registered a constant speed of 60. The vehicle's *actual* speed was:

$$S = \frac{3600}{62}$$

$$S = 58.06 \text{ mph } (km/h)$$

NOTE: In a speedometer accuracy test, it is recommended that the exact or actual speed result be used, i.e., do not round the speed up or down.

12.024 The following procedures are recommended when test skids are conducted:

a. Duplicate conditions as closely as possible.

b. Determine the accuracy of the speedometer as the true speed of the test vehicle must be known. Speedometer accuracy may be checked by radar or by determining the time it takes to travel a known distance, e.g., a measured mile or kilometer, at a constant speedometer reading. (See Formula 2-4.)

c. If possible, use a test vehicle equipped with a *shot marker*, a device which leaves a chalk mark on the roadway surface at the time and place of brake application. Measurements should then be taken from the spot where the chalk strikes the roadway surface. (See Fig. 12-6.)

d. For safety reasons, do not make test skids at a speed in excess of 35 mph (56 km/h).

e. If the speed limit allows, make test skids at 35 mph (56 km/h) or even at a substantially slower speed. It is not recommended that test skids be made at less than 15 mph (25 km/h) because there is a possibility of an excessively high resultant drag factor.

f. Travel in a straight path at a constant 3 to 5 mph (5 to 8 km/h) above the speed at which the test is to be made. Decelerate to the test speed. Apply the brakes quickly and hard and let the vehicle skid to a complete stop.

g. Measure the length of the skid mark of each tire. Include in the overall measurement any lead-in skid mark appearing as a shadow. (See Para's. 7.031 and 12.006, and Fig's. 7-29 and 12-1.)

Figure 12-6. A vehicle equipped with a *shot marker*. (Reproduced with permission of the manufacturer: *Pacific institute of Traffic Safety, Inc.*, PO Box 261, Westbank, B.C., Canada V0H 2A0)

12.025   There are two methods of determining the drag factor from test skids:
1. *Using the longest skid mark*
2. *Averaging skid marks*

12.026   Tests have shown use of the longest skid mark to be the more accurate method of determining coefficient of friction or drag factor. This is the method recommended.

12.027   In actual practice, both methods may be considered acceptable. Method 1, however, favors the accident vehicle because it tends to result in a somewhat lower drag factor than that obtained by Method 2.

12.028   It is recommended that the investigator round off to the nearest **higher** whole unit the final skid distance from a skid test or tests that will be used in a coefficient of friction or drag factor formula. Also, round **down** to the nearest whole number (expressed as a decimal fraction to two decimal places) the coefficient of friction (μ value) or drag factor (f

value) obtained from a test or tests. Example: An *f* value calculated at 0.753 would be rounded down to 0.75; an *f* value calculated at 0.608 would be rounded down to 0.60. These procedures together with the use of the longest skid mark in skid tests tend to support the practice of using always the minimum speed for the accident vehicle.

Longest Skid Mark

12.029   Use the following procedures to determine the drag factor based on the longest skid mark from test skids:
    a. Conduct two (2) test skids.
    b. Measure the length of the longest skid mark of each test.
    c. Calculate the drag factor from the longest skid mark of each test. (Use Formula 12 4 for this purpose.) Compare these two drag factors.
    d. If the drag factors are within 05 percent of each other, use the lower of the two in an applicable speed formula.
    e. If the first two test skids fail to produce drag factors that fall within 05 percent of each other, conduct further test skids until two drag factors are obtained that are within 05 percent.
    f. If circumstances are such that tests cannot or should not be made to produce results within the preferred 05 percent, two results within 10 percent can be considered acceptable.

12.030   When using a test vehicle other than the accident vehicle to perform test skids, ensure that the vehicle is one on which all wheels lock up at approximately the same time. If, however, it is known that the accident vehicle had less than 100 percent braking efficiency or capability, the degree of actual braking efficiency or capability should, if possible, be duplicated by using a vehicle with the same braking efficiency or capability.

Averaging Skid Marks

12.031   To average skid marks:
    a. Conduct two test skids.
    b. Average the skid mark lengths of each test.
    c. If the average skid mark lengths of the two tests are within 05 percent of each other, add the two averages together and divide by 2 to obtain the average skid distance to be used in the formula.

d. If these two tests fail to produce results that fall within 05 percent, conduct an additional test or tests until there are two consistent results, that is, results that fall within the preferred 05 percent. The average skid distance can then be placed into the drag factor formula (Formula 12-4) and the f value calculated.

e. If circumstances are such that tests cannot or should not be made to produce results within the preferred 05 percent, two results within 10 percent can be considered acceptable.

Example

Two test skids were made at 30 mph (48 km/h). Their average distances were not within 05 percent of each other. A third test was made, also at 30 mph (48 km/h), the average result of which was within 05 percent of the result of test 1. Therefore, the average distances of tests 1 and 3 should be used to determine the average skid distance. The average skid distance obtained from the average results of tests 1 and 3 was calculated to be 50 ft (15 m), rounded off to the nearest higher whole unit. Applying Formula 12-4 to the average results of tests 1 and 3, we calculate the drag factor as follows:

Formula 12-4

United States   *S.I.*

$$f = \frac{S^2}{30D} \qquad\qquad\qquad f = \frac{S^2}{254D}$$

where f = drag factor
   S = speed of vehicle in making test skids
   D = skid mark distance

$$f = \frac{30^2}{30 \times 50} \qquad\qquad f = \frac{48^2}{254 \times 15}$$

$$f = \frac{900}{1500} \qquad\qquad\qquad f = \frac{2304}{3810}$$

$$f = .60 \qquad\qquad\qquad\qquad f = .60$$

Drag Sleds

12.032   As explained in paragraphs 12.007 and 12.008, the drag factor (f), as applied to vehicle tires on a highway surface, is the ratio of the pounds (kilograms) of force (F) required to move an object at a ***constant*** speed over the surface to the weight (**W**) of the object being moved, i.e., *f* = **F/W**. It is the number of pounds (**kilograms**) force (pull) required to keep an object moving (sliding) at a constant speed that must be used in Formulae 12-1 and 12-2, not the initial or *static* force required to start the object moving from a position of rest.

12.033   It is obviously not practical to weigh a vehicle and move it along a roadway surface in order to determine the drag factor. The drag factor can be obtained more easily and just as accurately by using a much smaller and lighter object such as a tire and wheel (see Fig. 12-7), drag sled, or a piece of metal, depending upon the facilities available and the circumstances or requirements involved. Drag sleds can be purchased through commercial outlets or can be constructed with limited resources at home or at the office. A drag sled can be constructed from a part of a tire that is then filled with a heavy material such as concrete or lead. When a tire and wheel is to be used, select a tire and wheel from the accident vehicle if possible.

12.034   When using a drag sled, tire and wheel or other object to determine the drag factor:

  a. Weigh the unit with a scale.
  b. Use the same scale to pull the unit over the roadway surface.
  c. Conduct test pulls alongside the accident vehicle's skid mark, in the same direction as the vehicle was traveling.
  d. Carry out approximately 10 test pulls, preferably spaced over the entire length of the skid mark, as doing so will take into consideration all roadway surface factors including grade. Each test pull should be approximately 3 to 4 ft (1 to 1.5 m) in length.
  e. Record the amount of force (pull) in pounds or kilograms required to move the unit at a *constant* speed. Remember, it is the force required to keep the unit moving at a constant speed that must be recorded rather than the initial force (*static* force) required to move the unit from its at rest position.
  f. When measuring the drag factor where a *yaw mark* is involved, pull the drag sled or tire and wheel across the mark from the inside to the outside of the mark at the angle of the striations. The striations show the direction the vehicle was traveling and side-slipping. (Note the striation marks in Fig. 12-10.) Similarly, approximately 10 test pulls should be conducted over the length of the yaw mark, starting at the beginning of the mark and each pull

Figure 12-7. An alternate method of determinign the roadway coefficient of friction is to use a tire mounted on a wheel. Its weight (*A*) and the force (pull) to move it along the roadway surface (*B*) must be measured and then placed in Formula 12-2. A tire and wheel used by the accident vehicle is most suitable for this purpose.

should be approximately 3–4 ft (1–1.5 m) in length. This procedure will take into consideration all roadway surface factors, including grade or superelevation.

12.035   An investigator who uses a drag sled, tire and wheel or other device to determine drag factor should be knowledgeable about and properly trained in its use. This manual provides the basic information as to how to perform such tests. However, before examining roadway surfaces for drag factor, the student or investigator should properly qualify him- or herself by carrying out field tests with the unit to be used.

12.036   When an investigator wishes to carry out field tests in the proper use of a drag sled or tire and wheel, he or she should first determine the drag factor of the roadway surface by conducting test skids (in the manner described above) with a vehicle that is equipped with a shot marker. Knowing the correct drag factor, the investigator can then conduct several test pulls with the drag sled or other device to learn how to pull the unit so as to obtain similarly accurate results.

Example

From test skids, an investigator determines that the drag factor of a roadway surface is .65. By using Formula 12-5 below, he then calculates the force that will be required to pull his drag sled weighing 25 lbs (11 kg) over the same roadway surface. The calculated required force is 16.25 lbs (7.15 kg). He then conducts test pulls with the drag sled until the force consistently registers 25 lbs (11 kg) on the scale. Such agreement with the calculated required force would indicate that the test pulls were being properly done.

Formula 12-5

United States	*S.I.*
$F = Wf$	$F = Wf$

where F = force required to move unit at a constant speed
    W = weight of unit
    f = drag factor

$F = 25 \times .65$	$F = 11 \times .65$
$F = 16.25 \text{ lbs}$	$F = 7.15 \text{ kg}$

DRAG FACTOR ADJUSTMENTS

12.037   In cases where an accident occurs on a roadway that has a grade, no adjustment need be made to the calculated drag factor for use in a speed formula when drag factor tests are conducted at the same place, in the same direction and under the same conditions as applicable to the accident vehicle.

12.038   In cases where an accident occurs on a roadway that has a grade, an adjustment must be made to the calculated drag factor for use in a speed formula when drag factor tests are conducted on a level surface, or when tests are done with a vehicle traveling in a different direction or when the **Coefficient of Friction [Drag Factor] Guide** (Table 12-1, following para. 12.040) is used. An adjustment must also be made when an accident occurs on a level roadway and tests are carried out where there is a grade, or when the Guide is used. In such cases, the percent grade is added to/subtracted from the calculated drag factor.

Example 1 — Downgrade adjustment

A vehicle skidded on a roadway having a minus (−) 05 percent grade. Drag factor tests conducted on a nearby level surface yielded a drag factor of .61 for the level surface. The actual or adjusted drag factor at the place where the accident vehicle skidded would therefore be:

$$.61 \,^-\, .05 \,=\, .56 \;(\,f = .56)$$

Example 2 — Upgrade adjustment

A vehicle skidded on a roadway having an upgrade (+) of 05 percent. Drag factor tests conducted on a nearby level surface yielded a drag factor of .61 for the level surface. The actual or adjusted drag factor at the place where the accident vehicle skidded would therefore be:

$$.61 \,+\, .05 \,=\, .66 \;(\,f = .66)$$

12.039   Depending upon the seriousness of the accident and the extent to which the investigation is to be carried out, skid tests by themselves may sometimes preclude the necessity of further calculations or determinations in respect to the speed of an accident vehicle. For example, if an accident vehicle skidded 63 ft (19 m) on a roadway where the speed limit was 25 mph (40 km/h) and test skids conducted at 25 mph (40 km/h) measured only 40 ft (12 m), it becomes obvious that the accident vehicle was exceeding the speed limit. It is recommended, however, that proper speed calculations be completed whenever possible.

ROADWAY COEFFICIENT OF FRICTION [DRAG FACTOR] GUIDE

12.040   The **Roadway Coefficient of Friction [Drag Factor] Guide**, Table 12-1, incorporates the results of many tests conducted by different persons and organizations. There are many factors that nevertheless influence such results. When the Table is used, it is recommended that speed calculations be made using the extreme drag factors at either end of the

Table 12-1.
COEFFICIENT OF FRICTION (DRAG FACTOR) GUIDE
PREPARED FOR PASSENGER CARS AND SMALL, 4-WHEEL TRUCKS

PORTLAND CEMENT

	Polished or Glazed	Well-traveled	New, Coarse
Dry	.50–.75	.60–.75	.70–1.00
Wet	.35–.60	.45–.70	.50– .80

ASPHALT or TAR

	Excess Tar, Bleeding	Polished, Glazed	Well-traveled, Smooth	New, Coarse
Dry	.35–.60	.45–.75	.55–.80	.65–1.00
Wet	.25–.55	.40–.65	.40–.65	.45– .80

GRAVEL

Loose	Packed, Well-traveled
.40–.70	.50–.85

SNOW   **ICE**

	Cold, Loose	Cold, Packed	Cold, Frosted	Warm
Dry	.10–.25	.25–.55	.10–.25	
Wet	.30–.50	.30–.60		.05–.10

LARGE, COMMERCIAL–TYPE VEHICLES

As a general rule, you should base large, commercial-type vehicle drag factors on a range of 65%–75% of above the drag factors.

Caution· Use this table as a guide only.

[Courtesy of Rivers Traffic Consultants Ltd.]

164   REPORT No._____

ACCIDENT DATA	TEST DATA

ACCIDENT DATA

Date	Time	am / pm

Weather   Temp

Location

VEHICLE
Licence no.   VIN
Make   Yr.   Model
Odometer reading

TEST DATA

Date	Time	am / pm

Weather   Temp

Location

VEHICLE
Driver
Licence no.
Make   Yr.   Model
Odometer reading
Speed-O calibration date   19_____

ROADWAY	DIRECTION OF TRAVEL	ROADWAY	DIRECTION OF TRAVEL
Type		Type	
Condition		Condition	
Grade		Grade	

ACCIDENT SKID DATA

	Impending	Skid	Totals
RF	+	=	
LF	+	=	
RR	+	=	
LR	+	=	
	Total		
	Average		

Longest skid mark [_____]

TEST SKID DATA

Test no.	1	2	3
Speed			
RF			
LF			
RR			
LR			
Total			
Average			

Total for f value [_____]
f = _____%

YAW DATA
Length
Chord
Middle ordinate

MEASUREMENT METHOD
Tape   Wheel   Paced   Other

MEASUREMENT METhOD
Tape   Wheel   Paced   Other

FORMULAE *(United States)*

$$f = \frac{S^2}{30D}$$

$$R = \frac{C^2}{8M} + \frac{M}{2}$$

$$S = \sqrt{30\,Df} \quad \text{Skid}$$

$$S = 3.86 \sqrt{(f \pm e)\,R} \quad \text{Yaw}$$

Calculated Speed_____

FORMULAE *(Metric)*

$$f = \frac{S^2}{254D}$$

$$R = \frac{C^2}{8M} + \frac{M}{2}$$

$$S = \sqrt{254\,Df} \quad \text{Skid}$$

$$S = 11.27 \sqrt{(f \pm e)\,R} \quad \text{Yaw}$$

Investigator:_____

Figure 12-8. (Source: *Traffic Accident Investigators' Handbook* by Rivers. Courtesy Charles C Thomas, Publisher, Springfield, Illinois.)

range and at least one arbitrary drag factor in the middle of the extremes. Such calculations will give the investigator a good idea of the upper and lower speed limits involved as well as a probable average of these.

12.041–12.045 reserved.

SPEED FROM SKID MARKS

12.046 Speed from skid marks may be calculated as follows:

Formula 12-6

	United States	*S.I.*
(a)	$S = \sqrt{30\ Df}$	$S = \sqrt{254\ Df}$
or		
(b)	$S = 5.5\sqrt{Df}$	$S = 15.9\ \sqrt{Df}$

where S = speed
D = distance
f = drag factor

[NOTE: The examples in this manual use Formula 12-6(a). The speed calculations in Appendices B, and D are based on Formula 12-6(b). The results using either formula are, however, identical.]

Example

A vehicle skidded 69 feet (21 m) to a stop on a level roadway having a .75 drag factor. Its minimum speed at the commencement of its skid would have been:

$$S = \sqrt{30 \times 69 \times .75} \qquad\qquad S = \sqrt{254 \times 21 \times .75}$$
$$S = \sqrt{1552.50} \qquad\qquad\qquad S = \sqrt{4000.50}$$
$$S = 39.40 \qquad\qquad\qquad\quad S = 63.24$$
$$S = 40\ \text{mph} \qquad\qquad\qquad S = 63\ \text{km/h}$$

12.047 Formula 12-6 is suitable for calculating speed from skid marks when all wheels have braking capability or efficiency or when the accident vehicle is used for skid tests to determine the drag factor. However, if the accident vehicle had less than 100 percent braking capability or efficiency and the drag factor used assumes 100 percent capability or efficiency, such as when skid tests are performed with a four-wheel vehicle having braking capability or efficiency on all wheels or when the

Coefficient of Friction [Drag Factor] Table is used, then the formula must be modified to allow for the percentage decrease in braking capability or efficiency. For example, if the vehicle in the example in paragraph 12.046 had braking capability on only *three* of its *four* wheels, or 75 percent braking capability, then its speed may be estimated by using *Formula 12-7*.

Formula 12-7

United States	*S.I.*
$S = \sqrt{30\ Dfn}$	$S = \sqrt{254\ Dfn}$

where S = speed
D = skid distance
f = drag factor
n = percent braking capability or efficiency

$S = \sqrt{30 \times 69 \times .75 \times .75}$	$S = \sqrt{254 \times 21 \times .75 \times .75}$
$S = \sqrt{1164.37}$	$S = \sqrt{3000.37}$
$S = 33.68$	$S = 54.77$
$S - 33$ mph	$S = 54$ km/h

12.048   To estimate the speed of a motorcycle that has braking capability on its rear wheel only, use *Formula 12-7* with an n factor of .47.

Example

Same circumstances as outlined in paragraph 12.046.

United States	*S.I.*
$S = \sqrt{30 \times 69 \times .75 \times .47}$	$S = \sqrt{254 \times 21 \times .75 \times .47}$
$S = \sqrt{729.67}$	$S = \sqrt{1880.23}$
$S = 27.01$	$S = 43.36$
$S = 27$ mph	$S = 43$ km/h

12.049   When a skid mark traverses different kinds of roadway surfaces, the drag factor and the length of the skid on each surface must be known in order to calculate a vehicle's speed.

Formula 12-8

United States	*S.I.*
$S = \sqrt{30\ [(f_1 D_1) + (f_2 D_2)]}$	$S = \sqrt{254\ [(f_1 D_1) + (f_2 D_2)]}$

where S = speed

 f_1 = drag factor of first surface

 f_2 = drag factor of second surface

 D_1 = skid distance on first surface

 D_2 = skid distance on second surface

In instances where more than two surfaces are involved, enlarge the formula to include f_3 and D_3, etc.

Example

A vehicle skidded to a stop over two separate sections of roadway.

Section 1: Asphalt $f_1 = .70$

 $D_1 = 26$ ft (8 m)

Section 2: Concrete $f_2 = .75$

 $D_2 = 26$ ft (8 m)

Applying Formula 12-8.

$S = \sqrt{30 \times [(.70 \times 26) + (.75 \times 26)]}$ $S = \sqrt{254 \times [(.70 \times 8) + (.75 \times 8)]}$

$S = \sqrt{30\ (18.2 + 19.5)}$ $S = \sqrt{254\ (5.6 + 6)}$

$S = \sqrt{30 \times 37.7}$ $S = \sqrt{254 \times 11.6}$

$S = \sqrt{1131}$ $S = \sqrt{2946.40}$

$S = 33.63$ $S = 54.28$

$S = 33$ mph $S = 54$ km/h

12.050–12.055   reserved.

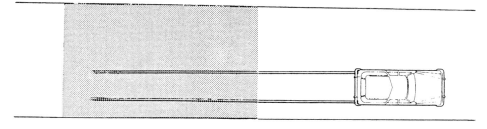

Figure 12-9. Continuous skid of different surfaces. The length of skid on each surface must be measured separately and the drag factor for each surface must be determined.

SPEED FROM YAW OR SIDESLIP

12.056   A vehicle that enters a curve at an excessive rate of speed, may go into yaw, sideslip and leave the highway. In so doing, yaw or sideslip marks will be left on the roadway surface. Under these circumstances, the vehicle's speed at the beginning or start of the yaw or sideslip marks may be calculated from the marks either (a) by using the marks themselves or (b) by plotting the vehicle's *center of mass* (C/M) *path* from the marks. The results are similar. For estimating purposes, a car's *center of mass* can be said to be approximately midway between its sides, at the center of the wheel base and one-third of the car's height above the ground.

12.057   It is the *radius* of the mark's arc (or center of mass path) rather than its length that allows for speed calculations. To determine the radius (See Figs. 12-10, 12-11 and 12-12), use the following directions:

   a. Start at the beginning of the yaw mark (or center of mass path) and measure a straight line from *a* to *b*. (See Figs. 12-10 and 12-12). This becomes the *chord* (C). Approximately the first one-third of the yaw mark (center of mass path) should be used for this purpose.

   b. Divide the *chord* length in half. Mark the mid point *c*. From point *c,* measure at a right angle to the arc of the yaw mark (center of mass path) and mark this point *d.* The distance from *c* to *d* is the *middle ordinate* (M).

   c. Always use the lead front tire mark if possible when calculating speed using a yaw mark by itself. If this mark is not adequate for some reason, use whatever other yaw mark is visible.

12.058   When a vehicle slides off a roadway in a curve, it may not always be possible or practical to use yaw marks for speed calculations. In these cases, the center line or roadway edge may be used to indirectly measure the radius of the vehicle's normal path of travel. The minimum speed at which the vehicle would have had to be travelling to slide off the roadway may be calculated using the path's radius, applying Formula 11-2. For example, if the roadway edge (*A*) in Figure 12-8 was calculated as having a radius of 406 feet (123.7 meters), the vehicle's path would have had a radius of 406 + 6 = 412 feet (123.7 + 1.83 = 125.53 meters).

12.059   The use of a yaw mark for speed calculations has certain limitations. Do not use Formula 12-9 if

   a. All wheels were not on the same surface.
   b. The vehicle was steered away from its yaw curve path.

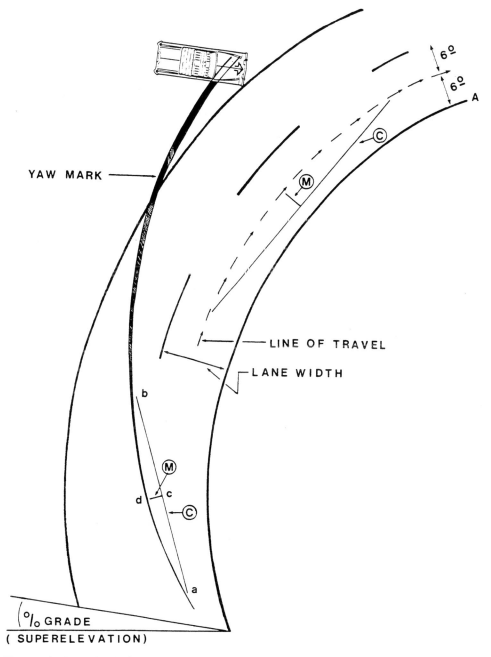

Figure 12-10. Method of plotting the radius of yaw marks, and the roadway line or path of travel. (Source: *Traffic Investigators' Handbook* by Rivers. Courtesy Charles C Thomas, Publisher, Springfield, Illinois.)

c. Brakes were applied.
d. The vehicle was a heavily loaded truck, particularly where there was a strong possibility of a load shift.

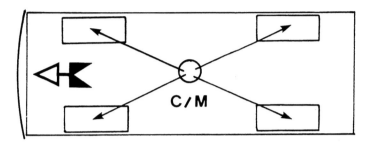

Figure 12-11. When using the center of mass to determine a vehicle's speed in yaw, measurements from the center of mass must be made to the contact area of each tire which in turn must be related to tire marks on the roadway.

Example

A vehicle entered a curve at an excessive rate of speed. It went into yaw leaving a yaw mark (or center of mass path) of 300 ft. (91m) in length. A *chord* was measured at 100 ft (30m) having a *middle ordinate* of 3 ft. (1m). The roadway had a +05 percent superelevation and a coefficient of friction of .70.

Step 1 — Calculate the radius

The radius may be calculated using Formula 11-2.

United States	*S.I.*

$$R = \frac{C^2}{8M} + \frac{M}{2} \qquad\qquad R = \frac{C^2}{8_M} + \frac{M}{2}$$

where R = Radius
$\quad C$ = Chord
$\quad M$ = Middle Ordinate

$$R = \frac{100^2}{8 \times 3} + \frac{3}{2} \qquad\qquad R = \frac{30^2}{8 \times 1} + \frac{1}{2}$$

$$R = \frac{10,000}{24} + 1.5 \qquad\qquad R = \frac{900}{8} + .5$$

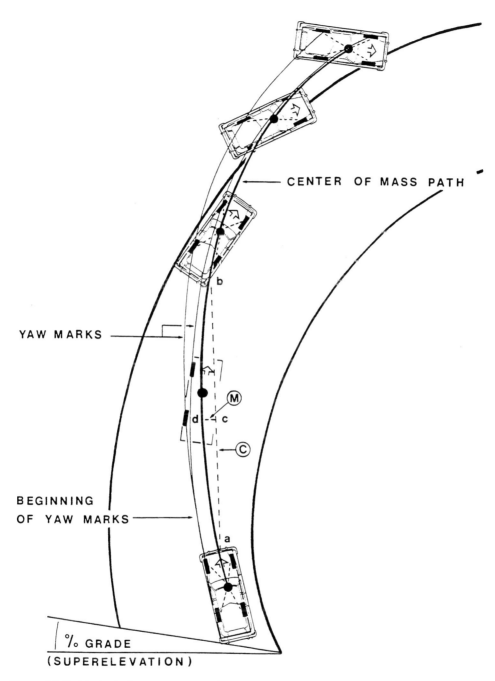

CENTER OF MASS PATH

YAW MARKS

BEGINNING
OF YAW MARKS

% GRADE
(SUPERELEVATION)

Figure 12-12. Method of plotting the radius of the center of mass path. (Source: *Traffic Accident Investigators' Handbook* by Rivers. Courtesy Charles C Thomas, Publisher, Springfield, Illinois.)

R = 416.67 + 1.5 R = 112.5 + .5

R = 418.17 R = 113 m

R = 418 ft.

Figure 12-13. A speedometer needle may stick at the speed the vehicle was travelling at the time of collision. Caution must be taken to ensure that the needle did not become jammed in its location because of broken or damaged internal parts or by broken face glass.

Step 2 — Calculate Speed

The speed of a vehicle in yaw, using a yaw mark or center of mass path, may be calculated using Formula 12-9.

Formula 12-9

$$\text{\textit{United States}} \qquad\qquad\qquad \text{\textit{S.I.}}$$

$$S = 3.86\sqrt{(f \pm e)\,R} \qquad\qquad S = 11.27\sqrt{(f \pm e)\,R}$$

where S = speed at commencement of yaw
f = drag factor
e = superelevation or bank of roadway
R = radius of yaw mark or center of mass path

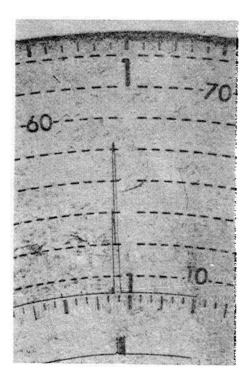

Figure 12-14. A segment of a tachograph chart. These charts can assist an investigator in determining the times involved in a trip and speeds registered. (Courtesy National Transportation Safety Board, Washington, D.C.)

$$S = 3.86 \sqrt{(.70 + .05)\ 418}$$

$$S = 3.86 \sqrt{.75 \times 418}$$

$$S = 3.86 \sqrt{313.5}$$

$$S = 3.86 \times 17.70$$

$$S = 68.32$$

$$S = 68 \text{ mph}$$

$$S = 11.27 \sqrt{(.70 + .05)\ 113}$$

$$S = 11.27 \sqrt{.75 \times 113}$$

$$S = 11.27 \sqrt{84.75}$$

$$S = 11.27 \times 9.21$$

$$S = 103.80$$

$$S = 103 \text{ km/h}$$

12.060–12.063   reserved.

SPEED FROM FALLS, FLIPS AND VAULTS

12.064   When a vehicle leaves a highway in a fall, flip or vault, its speed at the point of takeoff can be calculated if the horizontal and vertical distances of the vehicle's line of travel are determined. These measurements should be taken from the vehicle's approximate centers of mass

(*See* paragraph 12.056) at its point of takeoff and where it first lands. Subsequent rolls or bounces should be disregarded.

FALLS

12.065   A fall occurs in such instances as when a vehicle fails to negotiate a curve and is projected off the highway, frequently over an embankment. (*See* Fig. 12-15.) In these cases, any grade, plus or minus, of the roadway or area leading up to the point of takeoff must be considered.

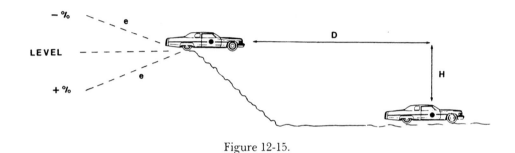

Figure 12-15.

12.066   If the takeoff area is level in a fall, use Formula 12-10.

Formula 12-10

United States	S.I.
$S = \dfrac{2.73\ D}{\sqrt{H}}$	$S = \dfrac{7.97\ D}{\sqrt{H}}$

where S = speed at takeoff (zero grade)
    D = horizontal distance
    H = Vertical fall distance

Example 1

A vehicle left the highway and fell to a point 80 ft. (24 m) horizontal distance and 10 ft. (3 m) below or vertical distance from the point of takeoff. Its speed at takeoff was:

United States	S.I.
$S = \dfrac{2.73 \times 80}{\sqrt{10}}$	$S = \dfrac{7.97 \times 24}{\sqrt{3}}$

$$S = \frac{218.4}{3.16} \qquad\qquad S = \frac{191.28}{1.73}$$

$$S = 69.11 \qquad\qquad S = 110.57$$

$$S = 69 \text{ mph} \qquad\qquad S = 110 \text{ km/h}$$

If the area leading up to the point of takeoff has a grade, use Formula 12-11.

Formula 12-11

$$S = \frac{2.73\,D}{\sqrt{H \pm (De)}} \qquad\qquad S = \frac{7.97\,D}{\sqrt{H \pm (De)}}$$

where S = speed

D = horizontal distance

H = vertical distance (fall or rise)

e = grade or elevation at takeoff area (added if plus percent grade; subtracted if minus percent grade

Example 2

Same circumstances as in Example 1, *except* the grade leading up to the point of takeoff was +05 percent.

$$S = \frac{2.73 \times 80}{\sqrt{10 + (80 \times .05)}} \qquad\qquad S = \frac{7.97 \times 24}{\sqrt{3 + (24 \times .05)}}$$

$$S = \frac{218.40}{\sqrt{10 + 4}} \qquad\qquad S = \frac{191.28}{\sqrt{3 + 1.2}}$$

$$S = \frac{218.40}{\sqrt{14}} \qquad\qquad S = \frac{191.28}{\sqrt{4.2}}$$

$$S = \frac{218.4}{3.74} \qquad\qquad S = \frac{191.28}{2.049}$$

$$S = 58.39 \qquad\qquad S = 93.35$$

$$S = 58 \text{ mph} \qquad\qquad S = 93 \text{ km/h}$$

Example 3

Same circumstances as Example 1, *except* the grade leading up to the point of takeoff was −05 percent.

$$\text{\textit{United States}} \qquad\qquad \text{\textit{S.I.}}$$

$$S = \frac{2.73 \times 80}{\sqrt{10 - (80 \times .05)}} \qquad\qquad S = \frac{7.97 \times 24}{\sqrt{3 - (24 \times .05)}}$$

$$S = \frac{218.4}{\sqrt{10 - 4}} \qquad\qquad S = \frac{191.28}{\sqrt{3 - 1.2}}$$

$$S = \frac{218.4}{\sqrt{6}} \qquad\qquad S = \frac{191.38}{\sqrt{1.8}}$$

$$S = \frac{218.4}{2.449} \qquad\qquad S = \frac{191.28}{1.342}$$

$$S = 89.17 \qquad\qquad S = 142.53$$

$$S = 89 \text{ mph} \qquad\qquad S = 142 \text{ km/h}$$

FLIPS AND VAULTS

12.067 A *sideways flip* or *vault* usually occurs when a vehicle strikes a substantial object such as a curb (*See* Fig. 12-16). When the centers of mass are *level* at the points of *takeoff* and *first landing or touch of ground,* use Formula 12-12.

Formula 12-12

United States	*S.I.*
$S = 3.86 \sqrt{D}$	$S = 11.27 \sqrt{D}$

where S = speed at takeoff
       D = distance between centers of mass

NOTE: Formulae 12-12 and 12-13 are intended for an assumed or an approximate takeoff angle of 45 degrees. These formulae are adequate for most speed calculations involving flips and vaults. In situations

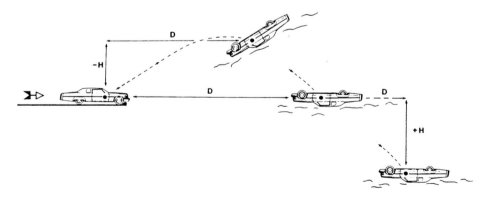

Figure 12-16.

where the angle of takeoff is either greater or lesser than a takeoff angle of 45 degrees, speed calculations using these formulae will be quite conservative. That is to say, the calculated speeds will be very much a minimum speed.

Example 1

A vehicle drove into an intersection at a high rate of speed and struck a curb. It flipped or vaulted through the air, *first* landing on a lawn. The center of mass at the point where the vehicle first landed was level with the center of mass at the takeoff point, and measured 30 ft (9.14 m). Its takeoff speed was:

United States	*S.I.*
$S = 3.86 \sqrt{30}$	$S = 11.27 \sqrt{9.14}$
$S = 3.86 \times 5.477$	$S = 11.27 \times 3.023$
$S = 21.14$	$S = 34.06$
$S = 21$ mph	$S = 34$ km/h

When a vehicle lands higher or lower than its takeoff point, measured between centers of mass, use Formula 12-13.

Formula 12-13

United States	*S.I.*
$S = \dfrac{3.86\ D}{\sqrt{D \pm H}}$	$S = \dfrac{11.27\ D}{\sqrt{D \pm H}}$

where S = speed at takeoff
$\quad D$ = distance between centers of mass
$\quad H$ = vertical fall or rise (subtracted in formula if landing is higher and added in formula if landing is lower)

Example 2

Same circumstances as in Example 1, *except* the landing was 10 ft (3 m) higher than its takeoff point, measured to the centers of mass.

United States	*S.I.*
$S = \dfrac{3.86 \times 30}{\sqrt{30 - 10}}$	$S = \dfrac{11.27 \times 9.14}{\sqrt{9.14 - 3}}$
$S = \dfrac{115.8}{\sqrt{20}}$	$S = \dfrac{103}{\sqrt{6.14}}$

$$S = \frac{115.8}{4.47} \qquad\qquad S = \frac{103}{2.478}$$

$$S = 25.90 \qquad\qquad\qquad S = 41.57$$

$$S = 25 \text{ mph} \qquad\qquad\quad S = 41 \text{ km/h}$$

Example 3

Same circumstances as Example 1, *except* the landing was 10 ft (3 m) lower than its takeoff point, measured to the centers of mass.

United States	*S.I.*

$$S = \frac{3.86 \times 30}{\sqrt{30 + 10}} \qquad\qquad S = \frac{11.27 \times 9.14}{\sqrt{9.14 + 3}}$$

$$S = \frac{115.8}{\sqrt{40}} \qquad\qquad\quad S = \frac{103}{\sqrt{12.14}}$$

$$S = \frac{115.8}{6.325} \qquad\qquad\quad S = \frac{103}{3.48}$$

$$S = 18.30 \qquad\qquad\qquad S = 29.60$$

$$S = 18 \text{ mph} \qquad\qquad\quad S = 29 \text{ km/h}$$

Appendix A

SUMMARY OF FORMULAE FOR LEVELS 1 AND 2 TRAFFIC ACCIDENT INVESTIGATION

DEFINITIONS

C = chord

D = distance

e = superelevation, slope or grade (Note: the symbol m is often used for this designation, but because m is also used for a variety of other factors, e is recommended for purposes of clarity.)

F = force in pounds (newtons)

f = drag factor

f_a = acceleration factor

L = length

M = middle ordinate

m = superelevation, slope or grade. (*See* also e.)

n = a percentage factor, e.g., the braking efficiency of a vehicle during a skid.

$_n$ = a subscript $_n$ indicates that the variable to which it is attached can theoretically occur an unlimited number of times

r = rise or fall in relation to measuring grade, slope or superelevation

R = radius

S = speed (a scalar quantity) measured in miles per hour (kilometers per hour)

$_f$ = subscript $_f$ designating *final* for the factor to which it is attached, e.g., S_f = final speed

$_o$ = subscript $_o$ designating *original* or *initial* for the factor to which it is attached, e.g., V_o = original or initial velocity

t = time

V = velocity (a vector quantity) measured in feet per second (meters per second)

W = weight measured in pounds (kilograms)

SPEED AND VELOCITY

United States   *S.I.*

Formula No. A1. Average velocity (V) or speed (S)

$$V = \frac{D}{t} \qquad\qquad V = \frac{D}{t}$$

$$S = \frac{D}{t} \qquad\qquad S = \frac{D}{t}$$

Formula No. A2. Converting speed in mph (km/h) to velocity in ft/s (m/s)

$$V = 1.466 \, S \qquad\qquad V = 0.278 \, S$$

Formula No. A3. Converting velocity in ft/s (m/s) to mph (km/h)

$$S = \frac{V}{1.466} \qquad\qquad S = \frac{V}{0.278}$$

SPEED BASED ON SLIDES OR SKIDS

Formula No. A4. Slide (skid) to a stop

(a) $\qquad S = \sqrt{30 \, Df} \qquad\qquad S = \sqrt{254 \, Df}$

or

(b) $\qquad S = 5.5 \, \sqrt{Df} \qquad\qquad S = 15.9 \, \sqrt{Df}$

Formula No. A5. Skid to a stop involving percentage braking

$$S = \sqrt{30 \, Dfn} \qquad\qquad S = \sqrt{254 \, Dfn}$$

Formula No. A6. Skid to a stop involving percentage braking and grade

$$S = \sqrt{30 \, D(fn \pm e)} \qquad\qquad S = \sqrt{254 \, D(fn \pm e)}$$

COMBINED SPEEDS

Formula No. A7. Skid to a stop over various surfaces or combining any number of speed losses

United States

$$S = \sqrt{30 \, [(D_1 f_1) + (D_2 f_2) + (\text{e.g., speed at impact})]}$$

S.I.

$$S = \sqrt{254 \, [(D_1 f_1) + (D_2 f_2) + (\text{e.g., speed at impact})]}$$

Formula No. A8. Combined speeds

United States and S.I.

$$S = \sqrt{S_1^2 + S_2^2 + \ldots S_n^2}$$

YAW OR SIDESLIP SPEED

Formula No. A9. Yaw speed (when superelevation is 10% or less)

$$S = 3.86 \sqrt{(f \pm e)\ R} \qquad\qquad S = 11.27 \sqrt{(f \pm e)\ R}$$

ACCELERATION FACTOR

Formula No. A10. Acceleration factor (positive or negative) if vehicle slows to a stop or starts from a stop

$$f = \frac{S^2}{30\ D} \qquad\qquad f = \frac{S^2}{245\ D}$$

DRAG FACTOR OR COEFFICIENT OF FRICTION

Formula No. A11. Drag factor or coefficient of friction using a drag sled (when weight and horizontal pull are known)

$$f = \frac{F}{W} \qquad\qquad f = \frac{F}{W}$$

TIME

Formula No. A12. Time to travel a known distance when travel is at a constant velocity or speed

(a)
$$t = \frac{D}{V} \qquad\qquad t = \frac{D}{V}$$
or

(b)
$$t = \frac{D}{S} \qquad\qquad t = \frac{D}{S}$$

Formula No. A13. Time to slow to a stop or accelerate from a stop if distance and acceleration factors (positive or negative) are known

$$t = .249 \sqrt{\frac{D}{f_a}} \qquad\qquad t = .045 \sqrt{\frac{D}{f_a}}$$

Formula No. A14. Time to slow to a stop if distance, acceleration and braking efficiency factors are known

$$t = .249 \sqrt{\frac{D}{f_a n}} \qquad\qquad t = .045 \sqrt{\frac{D}{f_a n}}$$

DISTANCE

Formula No. A15. Distance traveled at a constant speed or velocity when time is
known

(a) $D = Vt$ $D = Vt$

or

(b) $D = St$ $D = St$

Formula No. A16. Distance required to stop or to accelerate when speed and acceleration factor (positive or negative) are known

$$D = \frac{S^2}{30\, f_a}$$ $$D = \frac{S^2}{254\, f_a}$$

RADIUS

Formula No. A17

$$R = \frac{C^2}{8\,M} + \frac{M}{2}$$ $$R = \frac{C^2}{8\,M} + \frac{M}{2}$$

PERCENT GRADE, SLOPE, SUPERELEVATION

Formula No. A18

(a) $m = \dfrac{\text{rise}}{\text{run}}$ $m = \dfrac{\text{rise}}{\text{run}}$

or

(b) $e = \dfrac{r}{L} \times \dfrac{100}{1}$ $e = \dfrac{r}{L} \times \dfrac{100}{1}$

Appendix B

SPEED FROM SKID MARKS
IN MILES PER HOUR*

Based on Formulae No.'s 4(b) and 12-6(b)
For calculation examples, see paragraph 12.046

*Reproduced from Traffic Accident Investigators' Handbook by Rivers. Courtesy of Charles C Thomas, Publisher, Springfield, Illinois.

Appendix B
SPEED FROM SKID MARKS IN MILES PER HOUR

Coefficient of Friction (f)	Skid (feet)													
	5	6	7	8	9	10	11	12	13	14	15	16	17	18
0.05	2.750	3.012	3.254	3.479	3.690	3.888	4.078	4.260	4.434	4.601	4.763	4.919	5.071	5.218
0.10	3.889	4.260	4.602	4.919	5.218	5.500	5.768	6.024	6.270	6.507	6.736	6.957	7.171	7.379
0.15	4.763	5.218	5.636	6.025	6.390	6.732	7.064	7.379	7.680	7.970	8.250	8.521	8.783	9.037
0.20	5.500	6.025	6.508	6.957	7.379	7.777	8.157	8.520	8.868	9.203	9.526	9.839	10.141	10.436
0.25	6.149	6.736	7.276	7.778	8.250	8.695	9.120	9.526	9.915	10.289	10.650	11.000	11.339	11.667
0.30	6.736	7.379	7.971	8.521	9.037	9.526	9.991	10.435	10.861	11.271	11.665	12.050	12.421	12.781
0.35	7.276	7.970	8.609	9.203	9.762	10.285	10.791	11.271	11.731	12.174	12.602	13.015	13.416	13.805
0.40	7.778	8.521	9.203	9.839	10.436	11.000	11.536	12.049	12.541	13.015	13.469	13.914	14.342	14.758
0.45	8.250	9.037	9.761	10.436	11.069	11.665	12.236	12.780	13.302	13.804	14.289	14.758	15.212	15.653
0.50	8.696	9.526	10.290	11.000	11.667	12.298	12.898	13.472	14.022	14.551	15.059	15.556	16.035	16.500
0.55	9.121	9.991	10.792	11.537	12.237	12.897	13.528	14.129	14.706	15.261	15.796	16.316	16.818	17.305
0.60	9.526	10.436	11.272	12.050	12.781	13.469	14.129	14.758	15.360	15.940	16.500	17.041	17.566	18.075
0.65	9.915	10.862	11.732	12.542	13.303	14.019	14.706	15.360	15.987	16.591	17.171	17.737	18.283	18.813
0.70	10.290	11.272	12.175	13.015	13.805	14.547	15.261	15.940	16.591	17.217	17.820	18.407	18.973	19.523
0.75	10.651	11.667	12.602	13.472	14.289	15.059	15.797	16.500	17.173	17.822	18.447	19.053	19.639	20.208
0.80	11.000	12.050	13.015	13.914	14.758	15.554	16.315	17.041	17.736	18.406	19.052	19.677	20.283	20.871
0.85	11.339	12.421	13.416	14.342	15.212	16.032	16.817	17.565	18.282	18.973	19.635	20.283	20.907	21.513
0.90	11.667	12.781	13.805	14.758	15.653	16.500	17.305	18.074	18.812	19.523	20.207	20.871	21.513	22.137
0.95	11.987	13.131	14.183	15.162	16.082	16.951	17.779	18.570	19.328	20.058	20.757	21.443	22.103	22.744
1.00	12.298	13.472	14.552	15.556	16.500	17.391	18.241	19.052	19.830	20.579	21.296	22.000	22.677	23.335
1.05	12.602	13.805	14.911	15.941	16.907	17.820	18.691	19.523	20.320	21.087	21.824	22.543	23.237	23.911
1.10	12.899	14.130	15.262	16.316	17.305	18.238	19.131	19.982	20.798	21.583	22.341	23.074	23.784	24.473
1.15	13.189	14.447	15.605	16.682	17.694	18.650	19.561	20.431	21.265	22.068	22.841	23.592	24.318	25.023
1.20	13.472	14.758	15.941	17.041	18.075	19.052	19.982	20.871	21.723	22.543	23.331	24.100	24.841	25.562
1.25	13.750	15.062	16.269	17.393	18.448	19.442	20.394	21.301	22.171	23.008	23.815	24.597	25.354	26.089
1.30	14.022	15.361	16.591	17.737	18.813	19.827	20.798	21.723	22.610	23.463	24.282	25.084	25.856	26.605

Reproduced from Traffic Accident Investigators' Handbook by Rivers. Courtesy of Charles C Thomas, Publisher, Springfield, Illinois.

Coefficient of Friction (f)	Skid (feet)													
	19	20	25	30	35	40	45	50	55	60	65	70	75	80
0.05	5.361	5.500	6.149	6.736	7.276	7.778	8.250	8.696	9.121	9.526	9.915	10.290	10.651	11.000
0.10	7.581	7.778	8.696	9.526	10.290	11.000	11.667	12.298	12.899	13.472	14.022	14.552	15.062	15.556
0.15	9.285	9.526	10.651	11.667	12.602	13.472	14.289	15.062	15.798	16.500	17.174	17.822	18.448	19.053
0.20	10.721	11.000	12.298	13.472	14.552	15.556	16.500	17.393	18.241	19.053	19.831	20.579	21.301	22.000
0.25	11.987	12.298	13.750	15.062	16.269	17.393	18.448	19.445	20.395	21.301	22.171	23.008	23.816	24.597
0.30	13.131	13.472	15.062	16.500	17.822	19.053	20.208	21.301	22.341	23.335	24.287	25.204	26.089	26.944
0.35	14.183	14.552	16.269	17.822	19.250	20.579	21.827	23.008	24.131	25.204	26.233	27.224	28.179	29.103
0.40	15.162	15.556	17.393	19.053	20.579	22.000	23.335	24.597	25.797	26.944	28.045	29.103	30.125	31.113
0.45	16.082	16.500	18.448	20.208	21.827	23.335	24.750	26.089	27.362	28.579	29.746	30.869	31.952	33.000
0.50	16.952	17.393	19.445	21.301	23.008	24.597	26.089	27.500	28.842	30.125	31.355	32.538	33.680	34.785
0.55	17.780	18.241	20.395	22.341	24.131	25.797	27.362	28.842	30.250	31.595	32.885	34.127	35.324	36.483
0.60	18.570	19.053	21.301	23.335	25.204	26.944	28.579	30.125	31.595	33.000	34.347	35.644	36.895	38.105
0.65	19.328	19.831	22.171	24.287	26.233	28.045	29.746	31.355	32.885	34.347	35.750	37.100	38.402	39.661
0.70	20.058	20.579	23.008	25.204	27.224	29.103	30.869	32.538	34.127	35.644	37.100	38.500	39.851	41.158
0.75	20.762	21.301	23.816	26.089	28.179	30.125	31.952	33.680	35.324	36.895	38.402	39.851	41.250	42.603
0.80	21.443	22.000	24.597	26.944	29.103	31.113	33.000	34.785	36.483	38.105	39.661	41.158	42.603	44.000
0.85	22.103	22.677	25.354	27.774	29.999	32.070	34.016	35.856	37.606	39.278	40.882	42.425	43.914	45.354
0.90	22.744	23.335	26.089	28.579	30.869	33.000	35.002	36.895	38.696	40.417	42.067	43.655	45.187	46.669
0.95	23.367	23.974	26.804	29.362	31.715	33.904	35.961	37.906	39.756	41.524	43.220	44.851	46.425	47.948
1.00	23.974	24.597	27.500	30.125	32.538	34.785	36.895	38.891	40.789	42.603	44.342	46.016	47.631	49.193
1.05	24.566	25.204	28.179	30.869	33.342	35.644	37.806	39.851	41.796	43.655	45.437	47.153	48.808	50.408
1.10	25.144	25.797	28.842	31.595	34.127	36.483	38.696	40.789	42.780	44.682	46.507	48.262	49.956	51.595
1.15	25.709	26.377	29.490	32.305	34.894	37.303	39.566	41.706	43.741	45.686	47.552	49.347	51.079	52.754
1.20	26.262	26.944	30.125	33.000	35.644	38.105	40.417	42.603	44.682	46.669	48.575	50.408	52.178	53.889
1.25	26.804	27.500	30.746	33.680	36.379	38.891	41.250	43.481	45.604	47.631	49.576	51.448	53.254	55.000
1.30	27.335	28.045	31.355	34.347	37.100	39.661	42.067	44.342	46.507	48.575	50.558	52.467	54.308	56.089

Appendix B (Continued)
SPEED FROM SKID MARKS IN MILES PER HOUR

Coefficient of Friction (f)	Skid (feet)													
	85	90	95	100	105	110	115	120	125	130	135	140	145	150
0.05	11.339	11.667	11.987	12.298	12.602	12.899	13.189	13.472	13.750	14.022	14.289	14.551	14.809	15.062
0.10	16.035	16.500	16.952	17.393	17.822	18.241	18.651	19.052	19.445	19.831	20.208	20.579	20.943	21.301
0.15	19.639	20.208	20.762	21.301	21.827	22.341	22.843	23.334	23.816	24.287	24.750	25.204	25.650	26.089
0.20	22.677	23.335	23.974	24.597	25.204	25.797	26.377	26.944	27.500	28.045	28.579	29.103	29.618	30.125
0.25	25.354	26.089	26.804	27.500	28.179	28.842	29.490	30.125	30.745	31.355	31.952	32.538	33.114	33.680
0.30	27.774	28.579	29.362	30.125	30.869	31.595	32.305	33.000	33.680	34.347	35.002	35.644	36.275	36.895
0.35	29.999	30.869	31.715	32.538	33.341	34.127	34.893	35.644	36.379	37.099	37.806	38.500	39.181	39.851
0.40	32.070	33.000	33.904	34.785	35.644	36.483	37.303	38.105	38.891	39.661	40.417	41.158	41.887	42.603
0.45	34.016	35.002	35.961	36.895	37.806	38.696	39.566	40.416	41.250	42.067	42.868	43.655	44.427	45.187
0.50	35.856	36.895	37.906	38.891	39.851	40.789	41.706	42.603	43.481	44.342	45.187	46.016	46.831	47.631
0.55	37.606	38.696	39.756	40.789	41.796	42.780	43.741	44.682	45.603	46.507	47.393	48.262	49.117	49.956
0.60	39.278	40.417	41.524	42.603	43.654	44.682	45.686	46.669	47.631	48.575	49.500	50.408	51.301	52.178
0.65	40.882	42.067	43.220	44.342	45.437	46.507	47.552	48.575	49.576	50.558	51.521	52.467	53.395	54.308
0.70	42.425	43.655	44.851	46.016	47.153	48.262	49.347	50.408	51.448	52.467	53.466	54.447	55.411	56.358
0.75	43.914	45.187	46.425	47.631	48.808	49.956	51.079	52.178	53.254	54.308	55.343	56.358	57.356	58.336
0.80	45.354	46.669	47.948	49.193	50.408	51.595	52.754	53.888	55.000	56.089	57.158	58.207	59.237	60.249
0.85	46.750	48.105	49.424	50.707	51.959	53.182	54.378	55.547	56.692	57.815	58.917	59.998	61.060	62.104
0.90	48.105	49.500	50.856	52.178	53.466	54.724	55.972	57.158	58.336	59.492	60.625	61.737	62.830	63.904
0.95	49.424	50.856	52.250	53.607	54.931	56.224	57.487	58.724	59.935	61.122	62.286	63.429	64.552	65.655
1.00	50.707	52.178	53.607	55.000	56.358	57.684	58.980	60.249	61.492	62.710	63.904	65.077	66.229	67.361
1.05	51.960	53.466	54.931	56.358	57.750	59.109	60.437	61.737	63.010	64.258	65.482	66.684	67.864	69.024
1.10	53.182	54.724	56.224	57.684	59.109	60.500	61.859	63.190	64.493	65.770	67.023	68.253	69.461	70.649
1.15	54.378	55.954	57.487	58.980	60.437	61.859	63.250	64.610	65.943	67.249	68.530	69.787	71.022	72.237
1.20	55.547	57.158	58.724	60.249	61.737	63.190	64.610	66.000	67.361	68.695	70.004	71.288	72.550	73.790
1.25	56.693	58.336	59.935	61.492	63.010	64.493	65.943	67.361	68.750	70.112	71.447	72.758	74.046	75.312
1.30	57.815	59.492	61.122	62.710	64.258	65.770	67.249	68.695	70.112	71.500	72.862	74.199	75.512	76.803

Skid (feet)

Coefficient of Friction (f)	155	160	165	170	175	180	185	190	195	200	220	240
0.05	15.311	15.556	15.798	16.035	16.269	16.500	16.728	16.952	17.174	17.393	18.241	19.053
0.10	21.654	22.000	22.341	22.677	23.008	23.335	23.656	23.974	24.287	24.597	25.797	26.944
0.15	26.520	26.944	27.362	27.774	28.179	28.579	28.973	29.362	29.746	30.125	31.595	33.000
0.20	30.623	31.113	31.595	32.070	32.538	33.000	33.455	33.904	34.347	34.785	36.483	38.105
0.25	34.237	34.785	35.324	35.856	36.379	36.895	37.404	37.906	38.402	38.891	40.789	42.603
0.30	37.505	38.105	38.696	39.278	39.851	40.417	40.974	41.524	42.067	42.603	44.682	46.669
0.35	40.510	41.158	41.796	42.425	43.044	43.655	44.257	44.851	45.437	46.016	48.262	50.408
0.40	43.307	44.000	44.682	45.354	46.016	46.669	47.313	47.948	48.575	49.193	51.595	53.889
0.45	45.934	46.669	47.393	48.105	48.808	49.500	50.183	50.856	51.521	52.178	54.724	57.158
0.50	48.419	49.193	49.956	50.707	51.448	52.178	52.897	53.607	54.308	55.000	57.684	60.249
0.55	50.782	51.595	52.395	53.182	53.959	54.724	55.479	56.224	56.959	57.684	60.500	63.190
0.60	53.040	53.889	54.724	55.547	56.358	57.158	57.946	58.724	59.492	60.249	63.190	66.000
0.65	55.206	56.089	56.959	57.815	58.660	59.492	60.312	61.122	61.921	62.710	65.770	68.695
0.70	57.290	58.207	59.109	59.998	60.874	61.737	62.580	63.429	64.258	65.077	68.253	71.288
0.75	59.301	60.249	61.184	62.104	63.010	63.904	64.786	65.655	66.514	67.361	70.649	73.790
0.80	61.245	62.225	63.190	64.140	65.077	66.000	66.911	67.809	68.695	69.570	72.966	76.210
0.85	63.130	64.140	65.135	66.114	67.080	68.031	68.970	69.895	70.809	71.711	75.211	78.556
0.90	64.961	66.000	67.023	68.031	69.024	70.004	70.969	71.922	72.862	73.790	77.392	80.833
0.95	66.741	67.809	68.860	69.895	70.912	71.922	72.914	73.893	74.859	75.812	79.513	83.048
1.00	68.474	69.570	70.649	71.711	72.758	73.790	74.808	75.812	76.803	77.782	81.578	85.206
1.05	70.165	71.288	72.393	73.482	74.555	75.612	76.655	77.684	78.700	79.703	83.593	87.310
1.10	71.817	72.966	74.097	75.211	76.309	77.392	78.450	79.513	80.552	81.578	85.560	89.364
1.15	73.431	74.606	75.762	76.902	78.024	79.131	80.223	81.300	82.362	83.412	87.483	91.373
1.20	75.010	76.210	77.392	78.556	79.703	80.833	81.948	83.048	84.134	85.206	89.364	93.338
1.25	76.557	77.782	78.988	80.176	81.346	82.500	83.638	84.761	85.869	86.963	91.207	95.263
1.30	78.073	79.322	80.552	81.763	82.957	84.134	85.294	86.439	87.569	88.685	93.013	97.149

Appendix B (Continued)
SPEED FROM SKID MARKS IN MILES PER HOUR

Coefficient of Friction (f)	Skid (feet)										
	260	280	300	325	350	375	400	425	450	475	500
0.05	19.831	20.579	21.301	22.171	23.008	23.816	24.597	25.354	26.089	26.804	27.500
0.10	28.045	29.103	30.125	31.354	32.538	33.680	34.785	35.856	36.895	37.906	38.891
0.15	34.347	35.644	36.895	38.402	39.851	41.250	42.603	43.914	45.187	46.425	47.631
0.20	39.661	41.158	42.603	44.342	46.016	47.631	49.193	50.707	52.178	53.607	55.000
0.25	44.342	46.016	47.631	49.576	51.448	53.254	55.000	56.693	58.336	59.935	61.492
0.30	48.575	50.408	52.178	54.308	56.358	58.336	60.249	62.104	63.904	65.655	67.361
0.35	52.467	54.447	56.358	58.660	60.874	63.010	65.077	67.080	69.024	70.916	72.758
0.40	56.089	58.207	60.249	62.710	65.077	67.361	69.570	71.711	73.790	75.812	77.782
0.45	59.492	61.737	63.904	66.514	69.024	71.447	73.790	76.061	78.266	80.411	82.500
0.50	62.710	65.077	67.361	70.112	72.758	75.312	77.782	80.176	82.500	84.761	86.963
0.55	65.770	68.253	70.649	73.534	76.309	78.988	81.578	84.089	86.527	88.898	91.207
0.60	68.695	71.288	73.790	76.803	79.703	82.500	85.206	87.828	90.374	92.851	95.263
0.65	71.500	74.199	76.803	79.939	82.957	85.869	88.684	91.414	94.064	96.642	99.153
0.70	74.199	77.000	79.703	82.957	86.089	89.110	92.033	94.865	97.615	100.290	102.896
0.75	76.803	79.703	82.500	85.869	89.110	92.238	95.263	98.195	101.041	103.810	106.507
0.80	79.322	82.317	85.206	88.685	92.033	95.263	98.387	101.415	104.355	107.215	110.000
0.85	81.763	84.850	87.830	91.414	94.865	98.195	101.415	104.536	107.567	110.514	113.385
0.90	84.134	87.310	90.374	94.064	97.615	101.041	104.355	107.567	110.685	113.718	116.673
0.95	86.439	89.702	92.851	96.642	100.290	103.810	107.215	110.514	113.718	116.835	119.870
1.00	88.685	92.033	95.263	99.153	102.896	106.507	110.000	113.385	116.673	119.870	122.984
1.05	90.875	94.305	97.615	101.601	105.437	109.137	112.716	116.185	119.554	122.830	126.021
1.10	93.013	96.525	99.912	103.992	107.918	111.706	115.369	118.920	122.367	125.720	128.986
1.15	95.104	98.694	102.158	106.329	110.343	114.216	117.962	121.592	125.117	128.546	131.885
1.20	97.149	100.817	104.355	108.616	112.716	116.673	120.499	124.207	127.808	131.311	134.722
1.25	99.153	102.896	106.507	110.856	115.041	119.078	122.984	126.769	130.444	134.018	137.500
1.30	101.116	104.933	108.616	113.051	117.319	121.437	125.419	129.279	133.027	136.673	140.223

Appendix C

SPEED FROM SIDESLIP OR YAW MARKS IN MILES PER HOUR*

Based on Formula No.'s 9 and 12-9
For calculation examples, see paragraph 12.059

*Reproduced from Traffic Accident Investigators' Handbook by Rivers. Courtesy of Charles C Thomas, Publisher, Springfield, Illinois.

Appendix C

SPEED FROM SIDESLIP OR YAW MARKS IN MILES PER HOUR

Coefficient of Friction (f)	Radius (feet)											
	20	25	30	35	40	45	50	60	70	80	90	100
0.10	5.500	6.149	6.736	7.276	7.778	8.250	8.696	9.526	10.290	11.000	11.667	12.298
0.15	6.736	7.531	8.250	8.911	9.526	10.104	10.651	11.667	12.602	13.472	14.289	15.062
0.20	7.778	8.696	9.526	10.290	11.000	11.667	12.298	13.472	14.552	15.556	16.500	17.393
0.25	8.696	9.723	10.651	11.504	12.298	13.044	13.750	15.062	16.269	17.393	18.448	19.445
0.30	9.526	10.651	11.667	12.602	13.472	14.289	15.062	16.500	17.822	19.053	20.208	21.301
0.35	10.290	11.504	12.602	13.612	14.552	15.434	16.269	17.822	19.250	20.579	21.827	23.008
0.40	11.000	12.298	13.472	14.552	15.556	16.500	17.393	19.053	20.579	22.000	23.335	24.597
0.45	11.667	13.044	14.289	15.434	16.500	17.501	18.448	20.208	21.827	23.335	24.750	26.089
0.50	12.298	13.750	15.062	16.269	17.393	18.448	19.445	21.301	23.008	24.597	26.089	27.500
0.55	12.899	14.421	15.798	17.063	18.241	19.348	20.395	22.341	24.131	25.797	27.362	28.842
0.60	13.472	15.062	16.500	17.822	19.053	20.208	21.301	23.335	25.204	26.944	28.579	30.125
0.65	14.022	15.677	17.174	18.550	19.831	21.033	22.171	24.287	26.233	28.045	29.746	31.355
0.70	14.552	16.269	17.822	19.250	20.579	21.827	23.008	25.204	27.224	29.103	30.869	32.538
0.75	15.062	16.840	18.448	19.926	21.301	22.594	23.816	26.089	28.179	30.125	31.952	33.680
0.80	15.556	17.393	19.053	20.579	22.000	23.335	24.597	26.944	29.103	31.113	33.000	34.785
0.85	16.035	17.928	19.639	21.212	22.677	24.053	25.354	27.774	29.999	32.070	34.016	35.856
0.90	16.500	18.448	20.208	21.827	23.335	24.750	26.089	28.579	30.869	33.000	35.002	36.895
0.95	16.952	18.953	20.762	22.426	23.974	25.428	26.804	29.362	31.715	33.904	35.961	37.906
1.00	17.393	19.445	21.301	23.008	24.597	26.089	27.500	30.125	32.538	34.785	36.895	38.891
1.05	17.822	19.926	21.827	23.576	25.204	26.733	28.179	30.869	33.342	35.644	37.806	39.851
1.10	18.241	20.395	22.341	24.131	25.797	27.362	28.842	31.595	34.127	36.483	38.696	40.789
1.15	18.651	20.853	22.843	24.673	26.377	27.977	29.490	32.305	34.894	37.303	39.566	41.706
1.20	19.053	21.301	23.335	25.204	26.944	28.579	30.125	33.000	35.644	38.105	40.417	42.603
1.25	19.445	21.741	23.816	25.724	27.500	29.168	30.746	33.680	36.379	38.891	41.250	43.481
1.30	19.831	22.171	24.287	26.233	28.045	29.746	31.355	34.347	37.100	39.661	42.067	44.342
1.35	20.208	22.594	24.750	26.733	28.579	30.312	31.952	35.002	37.806	40.417	42.868	45.187

Reproduced from Traffic Accident Investigators' Handbook by Rivers. Courtesy of Charles C Thomas, Publisher, Springfield, Illinois.

Coefficient of Friction (f)	Radius (feet)											
	110	120	130	140	150	160	170	180	190	200	220	240
0.10	12.899	13.472	14.022	14.552	15.062	15.556	16.035	16.500	16.952	17.393	18.241	19.053
0.15	15.798	16.500	17.174	17.822	18.448	19.053	19.634	20.208	20.762	21.301	22.341	23.335
0.20	18.241	19.053	19.831	20.579	21.301	22.000	22.677	23.335	23.974	24.597	25.797	26.944
0.25	20.395	21.301	22.171	23.008	23.816	24.597	25.354	26.089	26.804	27.500	28.842	30.125
0.30	22.341	23.335	24.287	25.204	26.089	26.944	27.774	28.579	29.362	30.125	31.595	33.000
0.35	24.131	25.204	26.233	27.224	28.179	29.103	29.999	30.869	31.715	32.538	34.127	35.644
0.40	25.797	26.944	28.045	29.103	30.125	31.113	32.070	33.000	33.904	34.785	36.483	38.105
0.45	27.362	28.579	29.746	30.869	31.952	33.000	34.016	35.002	35.961	36.895	38.696	40.417
0.50	28.842	30.125	31.355	32.538	33.680	34.785	35.856	36.895	37.906	38.891	40.789	42.603
0.55	30.250	31.595	32.885	34.127	35.324	36.483	37.606	38.696	39.756	40.789	42.780	44.682
0.60	31.595	33.000	34.347	35.644	36.895	38.105	39.278	40.417	41.524	42.603	44.682	46.669
0.65	32.885	34.347	35.750	37.100	38.402	39.661	40.882	42.067	43.220	44.342	46.507	48.575
0.70	34.127	35.644	37.100	38.500	39.851	41.158	42.425	43.655	44.851	46.016	48.262	50.408
0.75	35.324	36.895	38.402	39.851	41.250	42.603	43.914	45.187	46.425	47.631	49.956	52.178
0.80	36.483	38.105	39.661	41.158	42.603	44.000	45.354	46.669	47.948	49.193	51.595	53.889
0.85	37.606	39.278	40.882	42.425	43.914	45.354	46.750	48.105	49.424	50.707	53.182	55.547
0.90	38.696	40.417	42.067	43.655	45.187	46.669	48.105	49.500	50.856	52.178	54.724	57.158
0.95	39.756	41.524	43.220	44.851	46.425	47.948	49.424	50.856	52.250	53.607	56.224	58.724
1.00	40.789	42.603	44.342	46.016	47.631	49.193	50.707	52.178	53.607	55.000	57.684	60.249
1.05	41.796	43.654	45.437	47.153	48.808	50.408	51.960	53.466	54.931	56.358	59.109	61.737
1.10	42.780	44.682	46.507	48.262	49.956	51.595	53.182	54.724	56.224	57.684	60.500	63.190
1.15	43.741	45.686	47.552	49.347	51.079	52.754	54.378	55.954	57.487	58.981	61.860	64.610
1.20	44.682	46.669	48.575	50.408	52.178	53.889	55.547	57.158	58.724	60.249	63.190	66.000
1.25	45.604	47.631	49.576	51.448	53.254	55.000	56.693	58.336	59.935	61.492	64.493	67.361
1.30	46.507	48.575	50.558	52.467	54.308	56.089	57.815	59.492	61.122	62.710	65.770	68.695
1.35	47.393	49.500	51.521	53.466	55.343	57.158	58.917	60.625	62.286	63.904	67.023	70.004

Appendix C (Continued)
SPEED FROM SIDESLIP OR YAW MARKS IN MILES PER HOUR

Radius (feet)

Coefficient of Friction (f)	260	280	300	325	350	375	400	450	500	550	600	650
0.10	19.831	20.579	21.301	22.171	23.008	23.816	24.597	26.089	27.500	28.842	30.125	31.355
0.15	24.287	25.204	26.089	27.154	28.179	29.168	30.125	31.952	33.680	35.324	36.895	38.402
0.20	28.045	29.103	30.125	31.355	32.538	33.680	34.785	36.895	38.891	40.789	42.603	44.342
0.25	31.355	32.538	33.680	35.056	36.379	37.656	38.891	41.250	43.481	45.604	47.631	49.576
0.30	34.347	35.644	36.895	38.402	39.851	41.250	42.603	45.187	47.631	49.956	52.178	54.308
0.35	37.100	38.500	39.851	41.479	43.044	44.555	46.016	48.808	51.448	53.959	56.358	58.660
0.40	39.661	41.158	42.603	44.342	46.016	47.631	49.193	52.178	55.000	57.684	60.249	62.710
0.45	42.067	43.655	45.187	47.032	48.808	50.521	52.178	55.343	58.336	61.184	63.904	66.514
0.50	44.342	46.016	47.631	49.576	51.448	53.254	55.000	58.336	61.492	64.493	67.361	70.112
0.55	46.507	48.262	49.956	51.996	53.959	55.853	57.684	61.184	64.493	67.641	70.649	73.534
0.60	48.575	50.408	52.178	54.308	56.358	58.336	60.249	63.904	67.361	70.649	73.790	76.803
0.65	50.558	52.467	54.308	56.526	58.660	60.718	62.710	66.514	70.112	73.534	76.803	79.939
0.70	52.467	54.447	56.358	58.660	60.874	63.010	65.077	69.024	72.758	76.309	79.703	82.957
0.75	54.308	56.358	58.336	60.718	63.010	65.222	67.361	71.447	75.312	78.988	82.500	85.869
0.80	56.089	58.207	60.249	62.710	65.077	67.361	69.570	73.790	77.782	81.578	85.206	88.685
0.85	57.815	59.998	62.104	64.640	67.080	69.434	71.711	76.061	80.176	84.089	87.828	91.414
0.90	59.492	61.737	63.904	66.514	69.024	71.447	73.790	78.266	82.500	86.527	90.374	94.064
0.95	61.122	63.429	65.655	68.336	70.916	73.405	75.812	80.411	84.761	88.898	92.851	96.642
1.00	62.710	65.077	67.361	70.112	72.758	75.312	77.782	82.500	86.963	91.207	95.263	99.153
1.05	64.258	66.684	69.024	71.843	74.555	77.172	79.703	84.537	89.110	93.460	97.615	101.601
1.10	65.770	68.253	70.649	73.534	76.309	78.988	81.578	86.527	91.207	95.659	99.912	103.992
1.15	67.249	69.787	72.237	75.186	78.024	80.763	83.412	88.471	93.257	97.809	102.158	106.329
1.20	68.695	71.288	73.790	76.803	79.703	82.500	85.206	90.374	95.263	99.912	104.355	108.616
1.25	70.112	72.758	75.312	78.387	81.346	84.201	86.963	92.238	97.227	101.973	106.507	110.856
1.30	71.500	74.199	76.803	79.939	82.957	85.869	88.685	94.064	99.153	103.992	108.616	113.051
1.35	72.862	75.612	78.266	81.462	84.537	87.504	90.374	95.856	101.041	105.973	110.685	115.205

Radius (feet)

Coefficient of Friction (f)	700	750	800	850	900	1000	1100	1200	1300	1400	1500	1600
0.10	32.538	33.680	34.785	35.856	36.895	38.891	40.785	42.603	44.342	46.016	47.631	49.193
0.15	39.851	41.250	42.603	43.914	45.187	47.631	49.955	52.178	54.308	56.358	58.336	60.249
0.20	46.016	47.631	49.193	50.707	52.178	55.000	57.684	60.249	62.710	65.077	67.361	69.570
0.25	51.448	53.254	55.000	56.693	58.336	61.492	64.493	67.361	70.112	72.758	75.312	77.782
0.30	56.358	58.336	60.249	62.104	63.904	67.361	70.643	73.790	76.803	79.703	82.500	85.206
0.35	60.874	63.010	65.077	67.080	69.024	72.758	76.309	79.703	82.957	86.089	89.110	92.033
0.40	65.077	67.361	69.570	71.711	73.790	77.782	81.578	85.206	88.685	92.033	95.263	98.387
0.45	69.024	71.447	73.790	76.061	78.266	82.500	86.527	90.374	94.064	97.615	101.041	104.355
0.50	72.758	75.312	77.782	80.176	82.500	86.963	91.207	95.263	99.153	102.896	106.507	110.000
0.55	76.309	78.988	81.578	84.089	86.527	91.207	95.659	99.912	103.992	107.918	111.706	115.369
0.60	79.703	82.500	85.206	87.828	90.374	95.263	99.912	104.355	108.616	112.716	116.673	120.499
0.65	82.957	85.869	88.685	91.414	94.064	99.153	103.992	108.616	113.051	117.319	121.437	125.419
0.70	86.089	89.110	92.033	94.865	97.615	102.896	107.918	112.716	117.319	121.748	126.021	130.154
0.75	89.110	92.238	95.263	98.195	101.041	106.507	111.706	116.673	121.437	126.021	130.444	134.722
0.80	92.033	95.263	98.387	101.415	104.355	110.000	115.369	120.499	125.419	130.154	134.722	139.140
0.85	94.865	98.195	101.415	104.536	107.567	113.385	118.920	124.207	129.279	134.159	138.868	143.422
0.90	97.615	101.041	104.355	107.567	110.685	116.673	122.367	127.808	133.027	138.049	142.894	147.580
0.95	100.290	103.810	107.215	110.514	113.718	119.870	125.720	131.311	136.673	141.832	146.810	151.625
1.00	102.896	106.507	110.000	113.385	116.673	122.984	128.986	134.722	140.223	145.516	150.624	155.563
1.05	105.437	109.137	112.716	116.185	119.554	126.021	132.172	138.049	143.686	149.110	154.343	159.405
1.10	107.918	111.706	115.369	118.920	122.367	128.986	135.282	141.293	147.067	152.619	157.975	163.156
1.15	110.343	114.216	117.962	121.592	125.117	131.885	138.323	144.473	150.372	156.049	161.526	166.823
1.20	112.716	116.673	120.499	124.207	127.808	134.722	141.298	147.580	153.607	159.405	165.000	170.411
1.25	115.041	119.078	122.984	126.769	130.444	137.500	144.211	150.624	156.774	162.692	168.402	173.925
1.30	117.319	121.437	125.419	129.279	133.027	140.223	147.067	153.607	159.879	165.914	171.737	177.370
1.35	119.554	123.750	127.808	131.742	135.561	142.894	149.869	156.533	162.924	169.075	175.009	180.748

Appendix C (*Continued*)
SPEED FROM SIDESLIP OR YAW MARKS IN MILES PER HOUR

Radius (feet)

Coefficient of Friction (f)	1700	1800	1900	2000
0.10	50.707	52.178	53.607	55.000
0.15	62.104	63.904	65.655	67.361
0.20	71.711	73.790	75.812	77.782
0.25	80.176	82.500	84.761	86.963
0.30	87.828	90.374	92.851	95.263
0.35	94.865	97.615	100.290	102.896
0.40	101.415	104.355	107.215	110.000
0.45	107.567	110.685	113.718	116.673
0.50	113.385	116.673	119.870	122.984
0.55	118.920	122.367	125.720	128.986
0.60	124.207	127.808	131.311	134.722
0.65	129.279	133.027	136.673	140.223
0.70	134.159	138.049	141.832	145.516
0.75	138.869	142.894	146.810	150.624
0.80	143.422	147.580	151.625	155.563
0.85	147.836	152.122	156.291	160.351
0.90	152.122	156.533	160.822	165.000
0.95	156.291	160.822	165.229	169.521
1.00	160.351	165.000	169.521	173.925
1.05	164.311	169.075	173.708	178.220
1.10	168.178	173.053	177.796	182.414
1.15	171.957	176.943	181.791	186.514
1.20	175.656	180.748	185.701	190.526
1.25	179.278	184.476	189.531	194.454
1.30	182.828	188.129	193.284	198.305
1.35	186.311	191.713	196.966	202.083

Appendix D

SPEED FROM SKID MARKS
IN KILOMETERS PER HOUR*

Based on Formulae No.'s 4(b) and 12-6(b)
For calculation examples, see paragraph 12.046

$$d = \frac{s_2}{254(fn \pm e)}$$

---

*Reproduced from Traffic Accident Investigators' Handbook by Rivers. Courtesy of Charles C Thomas, Publisher, Springfield, Illinois.

195

Appendix D

SPEED FROM SKID MARKS IN KILOMETERS PER HOUR

Coefficient of Friction (f)	Skid (meters)											
	1	2	3	4	5	6	7	8	9	10	11	12
0.05	3.555	5.028	6.158	7.111	7.950	8.709	9.407	10.056	10.666	11.243	11.792	12.316
0.10	5.028	7.111	8.709	10.056	11.243	12.316	13.303	14.221	15.084	15.900	16.676	17.418
0.15	6.158	8.709	10.666	12.316	13.770	15.084	16.293	17.418	18.474	19.473	20.424	21.332
0.20	7.111	10.056	12.316	14.221	15.900	17.418	18.813	20.112	21.332	22.486	23.584	24.632
0.25	7.950	11.243	13.770	15.900	17.777	19.473	21.034	22.486	23.850	25.140	26.367	27.540
0.30	8.709	12.316	15.084	17.418	19.473	21.332	23.041	24.632	26.126	27.540	28.884	30.168
0.35	9.407	13.303	16.293	18.813	21.034	23.041	24.887	26.606	28.220	29.746	31.198	32.585
0.40	10.056	14.221	17.418	20.112	22.486	24.632	26.606	28.443	30.168	31.800	33.352	34.835
0.45	10.666	15.084	18.474	21.332	23.850	26.126	28.220	30.168	31.998	33.729	35.375	36.948
0.50	11.243	15.900	19.473	22.486	25.140	27.540	29.746	31.800	33.729	35.553	37.289	38.947
0.55	11.792	16.676	20.424	23.584	26.367	28.884	31.198	33.352	35.375	37.289	39.109	40.848
0.60	12.316	17.418	21.332	24.632	27.540	30.168	32.585	34.835	36.948	38.947	40.848	42.664
0.65	12.819	18.129	22.203	25.638	28.664	31.400	33.916	36.258	38.457	40.537	42.516	44.406
0.70	13.303	18.813	23.041	26.606	29.746	32.585	35.196	37.626	39.909	42.067	44.121	46.083
0.75	13.770	19.473	23.850	27.540	30.790	33.729	36.431	38.947	41.309	43.544	45.669	47.700
0.80	14.221	20.112	24.632	28.443	31.800	34.835	37.626	40.224	42.664	44.972	47.167	49.264
0.85	14.659	20.731	25.390	29.318	32.779	35.907	38.784	41.462	43.977	46.356	48.619	50.781
0.90	15.084	21.332	26.126	30.168	33.729	36.948	39.909	42.664	45.252	47.700	50.028	52.253
0.95	15.497	21.917	26.842	30.995	34.653	37.961	41.002	43.833	46.492	49.007	51.399	53.685
1.00	15.900	22.486	27.540	31.800	35.553	38.947	42.067	44.972	47.700	50.280	52.734	55.079
1.05	16.293	23.041	28.220	32.585	36.431	39.909	43.106	46.083	48.878	51.522	54.037	56.439
1.10	16.676	23.584	28.884	33.352	37.289	40.848	44.121	47.167	50.028	52.734	55.308	57.768
1.15	17.051	24.114	29.533	34.102	38.127	41.766	45.112	48.227	51.153	53.920	56.551	59.066
1.20	17.418	24.632	30.168	34.835	38.947	42.664	46.083	49.264	52.253	55.079	57.768	60.336
1.25	17.777	25.140	30.790	35.553	39.750	43.544	47.033	50.280	53.330	56.215	58.959	61.580
1.30	18.129	25.638	31.400	36.258	40.537	44.406	47.964	51.276	54.386	57.328	60.126	62.800

Skid (meters)

Coefficient of Friction (f)	13	14	15	16	17	18	19	20	22	24	26	28
0.05	12.819	13.303	13.770	14.221	14.659	15.084	15.497	15.900	16.676	17.418	18.129	18.813
0.10	18.129	18.813	19.473	20.112	20.731	21.332	21.917	22.486	23.584	24.632	25.638	26.606
0.15	22.203	23.041	23.850	24.632	25.390	26.126	26.842	27.540	28.884	30.168	31.400	32.585
0.20	25.638	26.606	27.540	28.443	29.318	30.168	30.995	31.800	33.352	34.835	36.258	37.626
0.25	28.664	29.746	30.790	31.800	32.779	33.729	34.653	35.553	37.289	38.947	40.537	42.067
0.30	31.400	32.585	33.729	34.835	35.907	36.948	37.961	38.947	40.848	42.664	44.406	46.083
0.35	33.916	35.196	36.431	37.626	38.784	39.909	41.002	42.067	44.121	46.083	47.964	49.775
0.40	36.258	37.626	38.947	40.224	41.462	42.664	43.833	44.972	47.167	49.264	51.276	53.212
0.45	38.457	39.909	41.309	42.664	43.977	45.252	46.492	47.700	50.028	52.253	54.386	56.439
0.50	40.537	42.067	43.544	44.972	46.356	47.700	49.007	50.280	52.734	55.079	57.328	59.492
0.55	42.516	44.121	45.669	47.167	48.619	50.028	51.399	52.734	55.308	57.768	60.126	62.396
0.60	44.406	46.083	47.700	49.264	50.781	52.253	53.685	55.079	57.768	60.336	62.800	65.171
0.65	46.220	47.964	49.648	51.276	52.854	54.386	55.877	57.323	60.126	62.800	65.364	67.832
0.70	47.964	49.775	51.522	53.212	54.849	56.439	57.986	59.492	62.396	65.171	67.832	70.392
0.75	49.648	51.522	53.330	55.079	56.774	58.420	60.021	61.580	64.586	67.458	70.212	72.863
0.80	51.276	53.212	55.079	56.886	58.636	60.336	61.990	63.600	66.704	69.670	72.515	75.253
0.85	52.854	54.849	56.774	58.636	60.441	62.193	63.897	65.557	68.757	71.815	74.747	77.569
0.90	54.386	56.439	58.420	60.336	62.193	63.996	65.750	67.458	70.751	73.897	76.914	79.817
0.95	55.877	57.986	60.021	61.990	63.897	65.750	67.552	69.306	72.689	75.921	79.022	82.005
1.00	57.328	59.492	61.580	63.600	65.557	67.458	69.306	71.107	74.578	77.894	81.074	84.135
1.05	58.744	60.962	63.101	65.171	67.176	69.124	71.018	72.863	76.419	79.817	83.077	86.213
1.10	60.126	62.396	64.586	66.704	68.757	70.751	72.689	74.578	78.218	81.696	85.032	88.241
1.15	61.478	63.798	66.038	68.203	70.302	72.341	74.323	76.254	79.976	83.532	86.943	90.225
1.20	62.800	65.171	67.458	69.670	71.815	73.897	75.921	77.894	81.696	85.328	88.813	92.165
1.25	64.095	66.514	68.849	71.107	73.295	75.420	77.487	79.500	83.381	87.088	90.644	94.066
1.30	65.364	67.832	70.212	72.515	74.747	76.914	79.022	81.074	85.032	88.813	92.439	95.929

Traffic Accident Investigators' Manual

Appendix D (*Continued*)
SPEED FROM SKID MARKS IN KILOMETERS PER HOUR

Skid (meters)

Coefficient of Friction (*f*)	30	32	34	36	38	40	42	44	46	48	50	52
0.05	19.473	20.112	20.731	21.332	21.917	22.486	23.041	23.584	24.114	24.632	25.140	25.638
0.10	27.540	28.443	29.318	30.168	30.995	31.800	32.585	33.352	34.102	34.835	35.553	36.258
0.15	33.729	34.835	35.907	36.948	37.961	38.947	39.909	40.848	41.766	42.664	43.544	44.406
0.20	38.947	40.224	41.462	42.664	43.833	44.972	46.083	47.167	48.227	49.264	50.280	51.276
0.25	43.544	44.972	46.356	47.700	49.007	50.280	51.522	52.734	53.920	55.079	56.215	57.328
0.30	47.700	49.264	50.781	52.253	53.685	55.079	56.439	57.768	59.066	60.336	61.580	62.800
0.35	51.522	53.212	54.849	56.439	57.986	59.492	60.962	62.396	63.798	65.171	66.514	67.832
0.40	55.079	56.886	58.636	60.336	61.990	63.600	65.171	66.704	68.203	69.670	71.107	72.515
0.45	58.420	60.336	62.193	63.996	65.750	67.458	69.124	70.751	72.341	73.897	75.420	76.914
0.50	61.580	63.600	65.557	67.458	69.306	71.107	72.863	74.578	76.254	77.894	79.500	81.074
0.55	64.586	66.704	68.757	70.751	72.689	74.578	76.419	78.218	79.976	81.696	83.380	85.032
0.60	67.458	69.670	71.815	73.897	75.921	77.894	79.817	81.696	83.532	85.328	87.088	88.813
0.65	70.212	72.515	74.747	76.914	79.022	81.074	83.077	85.032	86.943	88.813	90.644	92.439
0.70	72.863	75.253	77.549	79.817	82.005	84.135	86.213	88.241	90.225	92.165	94.066	95.929
0.75	75.420	77.894	80.291	82.619	84.883	87.088	89.239	91.339	93.391	95.400	97.367	99.295
0.80	77.894	80.448	82.924	85.328	87.667	89.944	92.165	94.334	96.454	98.529	100.560	102.552
0.85	80.291	82.924	85.476	87.954	90.365	92.712	95.002	97.237	99.423	101.561	103.655	105.708
0.90	82.619	85.328	87.954	90.504	92.984	95.400	97.756	100.056	102.305	104.505	106.660	108.773
0.95	84.883	87.667	90.365	92.984	95.532	98.014	100.435	102.798	105.109	107.369	109.583	111.753
1.00	87.088	89.944	92.712	95.400	98.014	100.560	103.044	105.469	107.839	110.158	112.430	114.657
1.05	89.239	92.165	95.002	97.756	100.435	103.044	105.588	108.073	110.502	112.879	115.206	117.488
1.10	91.339	94.334	97.237	100.056	102.798	105.469	108.073	110.616	113.103	115.535	117.918	120.253
1.15	93.391	96.454	99.423	102.305	105.109	107.839	110.502	113.103	115.644	118.132	120.567	122.955
1.20	95.400	98.529	101.561	104.505	107.369	110.158	112.879	115.535	118.132	120.673	123.161	125.600
1.25	97.367	100.560	103.655	106.660	109.583	112.430	115.206	117.918	120.568	123.161	125.701	128.190
1.30	99.295	102.552	105.708	108.773	111.753	114.657	117.488	120.253	122.955	125.600	128.190	130.729

Skid (meters)

Coefficient of Friction (f)	54	56	58	60	62	64	66	68	70	75	80	85
0.05	26.126	26.606	27.077	27.540	27.995	28.443	28.884	29.318	29.746	30.790	31.800	32.779
0.10	36.948	37.626	38.292	38.947	39.591	40.224	40.843	41.462	42.067	43.544	44.972	46.356
0.15	45.252	46.083	46.898	47.700	48.488	49.264	50.028	50.781	51.522	53.330	55.079	56.774
0.20	52.253	53.212	54.153	55.079	55.990	56.886	57.768	58.636	59.492	61.580	63.600	65.557
0.25	58.420	59.492	60.545	61.580	62.598	63.600	64.586	65.557	66.514	68.849	71.107	73.295
0.30	63.996	65.171	66.324	67.458	68.573	69.670	70.751	71.815	72.863	75.420	77.894	80.291
0.35	69.124	70.392	71.638	72.863	74.067	75.253	76.419	77.569	78.701	81.463	84.135	86.724
0.40	73.897	75.253	76.585	77.894	79.181	80.448	81.696	82.924	84.135	87.088	89.944	92.712
0.45	78.379	79.817	81.230	82.619	83.985	85.328	86.651	87.954	89.239	92.371	95.400	98.336
0.50	82.619	84.135	85.624	87.088	88.527	89.944	91.339	92.712	94.066	97.367	100.560	103.655
0.55	86.651	88.241	89.803	91.339	92.848	94.334	95.797	97.237	98.657	102.120	105.469	108.715
0.60	90.504	92.165	93.797	95.400	96.977	98.529	100.056	101.561	103.044	106.660	110.158	113.549
0.65	94.200	95.929	97.627	99.295	100.937	102.552	104.141	105.708	107.251	111.016	114.657	118.185
0.70	97.756	99.550	101.312	103.044	104.747	106.423	108.072	109.698	111.300	115.206	118.985	122.647
0.75	101.187	103.044	104.868	106.660	108.424	110.158	111.866	113.549	115.206	119.250	123.161	126.951
0.80	104.505	106.423	108.307	110.158	111.979	113.771	115.535	117.273	118.985	123.161	127.200	131.115
0.85	107.722	109.698	111.640	113.549	115.426	117.273	119.091	120.882	122.647	126.951	131.115	135.150
0.90	110.845	112.879	114.877	116.841	118.772	120.673	122.544	124.386	126.202	130.632	134.916	139.068
0.95	113.882	115.972	118.025	120.042	122.027	123.979	125.901	127.795	129.661	134.211	138.613	142.879
1.00	116.841	118.985	121.091	123.161	125.197	127.200	129.172	131.115	133.029	137.698	142.214	146.591
1.05	119.726	121.923	124.081	126.202	128.288	130.341	132.362	134.353	136.314	141.099	145.726	150.211
1.10	122.544	124.792	127.001	129.172	131.307	133.408	135.477	137.514	139.522	144.419	149.155	153.746
1.15	125.298	127.597	129.855	132.075	134.259	136.407	138.522	140.605	142.658	147.665	152.507	157.201
1.20	127.993	130.341	132.648	134.916	137.146	139.341	141.501	143.629	145.726	150.841	155.788	160.582
1.25	130.632	133.029	135.384	137.698	139.974	142.214	144.419	146.591	148.731	153.951	159.000	163.893
1.30	133.219	135.663	138.065	140.425	142.746	145.030	147.279	149.494	151.676	157.000	162.149	167.139

Appendix D (Continued)
SPEED FROM SKID MARKS IN KILOMETERS PER HOUR

Coefficient of Friction (f)	Skid (meters)							
	90	95	100	110	120	130	140	150
0.05	33.729	34.653	35.553	37.289	38.946	40.537	42.067	43.544
0.10	47.700	49.007	50.280	52.734	55.079	57.328	59.492	61.580
0.15	58.420	60.021	61.580	64.586	67.458	70.212	72.863	75.420
0.20	67.458	69.306	71.107	74.578	77.894	81.074	84.135	87.088
0.25	75.420	77.487	79.500	83.380	87.088	90.644	94.066	97.367
0.30	82.619	84.883	87.088	91.339	95.400	99.295	103.044	106.660
0.35	89.239	91.684	94.066	98.657	103.044	107.251	111.300	115.206
0.40	95.400	98.014	100.560	105.469	110.158	114.657	118.985	123.161
0.45	101.187	103.960	106.660	111.866	116.841	121.612	126.202	130.632
0.50	106.660	109.583	112.430	117.918	123.161	128.190	133.029	137.698
0.55	111.866	114.932	117.918	123.673	129.172	134.447	139.522	144.419
0.60	116.841	120.042	123.161	129.172	134.916	140.425	145.726	150.841
0.65	121.612	124.944	128.190	134.447	140.425	146.159	151.676	157.000
0.70	126.202	129.661	133.029	139.522	145.726	151.676	157.402	162.927
0.75	130.632	134.211	137.698	144.419	150.841	157.000	162.927	168.645
0.80	134.916	138.613	142.214	149.155	155.788	162.149	168.270	174.176
0.85	139.068	142.879	146.591	153.746	160.582	167.139	173.449	179.536
0.90	143.100	147.021	150.841	158.203	165.238	171.985	178.477	184.741
0.95	147.021	151.050	154.974	162.538	169.765	176.698	183.368	189.804
1.00	150.841	154.974	159.000	166.761	174.176	181.288	188.131	194.734
1.05	154.566	158.801	162.927	170.879	178.477	185.765	192.777	199.543
1.10	158.203	162.538	166.761	174.900	182.677	190.136	197.314	204.239
1.15	161.759	166.191	170.508	178.831	186.783	194.410	201.748	208.829
1.20	165.238	169.766	174.176	182.677	190.800	198.591	206.088	213.321
1.25	168.645	173.266	177.767	186.444	194.734	202.686	210.337	217.720
1.30	171.985	176.698	181.288	190.136	198.591	206.700	214.503	222.031

Appendix E

SPEED FROM SIDESLIP OR YAW MARKS
IN KILOMETERS PER HOUR*

Based on Formula No.'s 9 and 12-9
For calculation examples, see paragraph 12.059

---

*Reproduced from Traffic Accident Investigators' Handbook by Rivers. Courtesy of Charles C Thomas, Publisher, Springfield, Illinois.

Appendix E
SPEED FROM SLIDESLIP OR YAW MARKS IN KILOMETERS PER HOUR

Coefficient of Friction (*f*)	Radius (*meters*)											
	8	10	12	14	16	18	20	22	24	26	30	35
0.05	7.128	7.969	8.730	9.429	10.080	10.692	11.270	11.820	12.346	12.850	13.803	14.909
0.10	10.080	11.270	12.346	13.335	14.256	15.120	15.938	16.716	17.459	18.172	19.520	21.084
0.15	12.346	13.803	15.120	16.332	17.459	18.518	19.520	20.473	21.383	22.256	23.907	25.823
0.20	14.256	15.938	17.459	18.858	20.160	21.383	22.540	23.640	24.691	25.700	27.606	29.818
0.25	15.938	17.819	19.520	21.084	22.540	23.907	25.200	26.430	27.606	28.733	30.864	33.337
0.30	17.459	19.520	21.383	23.097	24.691	26.189	27.606	28.953	30.241	31.475	33.810	36.519
0.35	18.858	21.084	23.097	24.947	26.670	28.287	29.818	31.273	32.664	33.997	36.519	39.445
0.40	20.160	22.540	24.691	26.670	28.511	30.241	31.876	33.432	34.919	36.345	39.040	42.168
0.45	21.383	23.907	26.189	28.287	30.241	32.075	33.810	35.460	37.037	38.549	41.409	44.726
0.50	22.540	25.200	27.606	29.818	31.876	33.810	35.639	37.378	39.040	40.635	43.649	47.146
0.55	23.640	26.430	28.953	31.273	33.432	35.460	37.378	39.203	40.946	42.618	45.779	49.447
0.60	24.691	27.606	30.241	32.664	34.919	37.037	39.040	40.946	42.767	44.513	47.815	51.646
0.65	25.700	28.733	31.475	33.997	36.345	38.549	40.635	42.618	44.513	46.331	49.767	53.754
0.70	26.670	29.818	32.664	35.281	37.717	40.005	42.168	44.227	46.193	48.079	51.646	55.784
0.75	27.606	30.864	33.810	36.519	39.040	41.409	43.649	45.779	47.815	49.767	53.458	57.742
0.80	28.511	31.876	34.919	37.717	40.321	42.767	45.080	47.280	49.383	51.399	55.211	59.635
0.85	29.389	32.857	35.993	38.877	41.562	44.083	46.467	48.735	50.902	52.981	56.911	61.471
0.90	30.241	33.810	37.037	40.005	42.767	45.361	47.815	50.148	52.378	54.517	58.561	63.253
0.95	31.069	34.736	38.052	41.101	43.939	46.604	49.125	51.523	53.814	56.011	60.165	64.986
1.00	31.876	35.639	39.040	42.168	45.080	47.815	50.401	52.861	55.211	57.466	61.728	66.674
1.05	32.664	36.519	40.005	43.210	46.193	48.995	51.646	54.166	56.575	58.885	63.253	68.321
1.10	33.432	37.378	40.946	44.227	47.280	50.148	52.861	55.441	57.906	60.271	64.741	69.929
1.15	34.184	38.218	41.866	45.221	48.343	51.275	54.049	56.687	59.208	61.625	66.196	71.500
1.20	34.919	39.040	42.767	46.193	49.383	52.378	55.211	57.906	60.481	62.951	67.620	73.038
1.25	35.639	39.845	43.649	47.146	50.401	53.458	56.350	59.100	61.728	64.249	69.014	74.544
1.30	36.345	40.635	44.513	48.079	51.399	54.517	57.466	60.271	62.951	65.521	70.381	76.020

Radius (meters)

Coefficient of Friction (f)	40	45	50	55	60	65	70	75	80	85	90	95
0.05	15.938	16.905	17.819	18.689	19.520	20.317	21.084	21.824	22.540	23.234	23.907	24.562
0.10	22.540	23.907	25.200	26.430	27.606	28.733	29.815	30.864	31.876	32.857	33.810	34.736
0.15	27.606	29.280	30.864	32.371	33.810	35.191	36.513	37.801	39.040	40.242	41.409	42.543
0.20	31.876	33.810	35.639	37.378	39.040	40.635	42.163	43.649	45.080	46.467	47.815	49.125
0.25	35.639	37.801	39.845	41.790	43.649	45.431	47.145	48.801	50.401	51.952	53.458	54.923
0.30	39.040	41.409	43.649	45.779	47.815	49.767	51.646	53.458	55.211	56.911	58.561	60.165
0.35	42.168	44.726	47.146	49.447	51.646	53.754	55.784	57.742	59.635	61.471	63.253	64.986
0.40	45.080	47.815	50.401	52.861	55.211	57.466	59.635	61.728	63.753	65.715	67.620	69.473
0.45	47.815	50.715	53.458	56.068	58.561	60.952	63.253	65.473	67.620	69.701	71.722	73.687
0.50	50.401	53.458	56.350	59.100	61.728	64.249	66.674	69.014	71.278	73.471	75.601	77.673
0.55	52.861	56.068	59.100	61.985	64.741	67.385	69.929	72.383	74.757	77.057	79.291	81.464
0.60	55.211	58.561	61.728	64.741	67.620	70.381	73.038	75.601	78.081	80.484	82.817	85.087
0.65	57.466	60.952	64.249	67.385	70.381	73.255	76.020	78.688	81.269	83.770	86.199	88.561
0.70	59.635	63.253	66.674	69.929	73.038	76.020	78.890	81.659	84.337	86.933	89.453	91.904
0.75	61.728	65.473	69.014	72.383	75.601	78.688	81.659	84.525	87.297	89.984	92.592	95.130
0.80	63.753	67.620	71.278	74.757	78.081	81.269	84.337	87.297	90.160	92.935	95.629	98.250
0.85	65.715	69.701	73.471	77.057	80.484	83.770	86.935	89.984	92.935	95.795	98.572	101.273
0.90	67.620	71.722	75.601	79.291	82.817	86.199	89.453	92.592	95.629	98.572	101.430	104.209
0.95	69.473	73.687	77.673	81.464	85.087	88.561	91.904	95.130	98.250	101.273	104.209	107.065
1.00	71.278	75.601	79.691	83.581	87.297	90.862	94.293	97.601	100.802	103.904	106.917	109.846
1.05	73.038	77.468	81.659	85.645	89.453	93.105	96.620	100.011	103.291	106.470	109.557	112.559
1.10	74.757	79.291	83.581	87.660	91.558	95.296	98.894	102.365	105.722	108.976	112.135	115.208
1.15	76.437	81.074	85.459	89.630	93.616	97.438	101.116	104.665	108.098	111.425	114.655	117.797
1.20	78.081	82.817	87.297	91.558	95.629	99.534	103.291	106.917	110.423	113.821	117.121	120.331
1.25	79.691	84.525	89.097	93.446	97.601	101.586	105.421	109.121	112.700	116.169	119.536	122.812
1.30	81.269	86.199	90.862	95.296	99.534	103.598	107.509	111.282	114.932	118.469	121.904	125.244

Traffic Accident Investigators' Manual

Appendix E (Continued)
SPEED FROM SLIDESLIP OR YAW MARKS IN KILOMETERS PER HOUR

Radius (meters)

Coefficient of Friction (f)	100	110	120	130	140	150	160	170	180	190	200	220
0.05	25.200	26.430	27.606	28.733	29.818	30.864	31.876	32.857	33.810	34.736	35.639	37.378
0.10	35.639	37.378	39.040	40.635	42.168	43.649	45.080	46.467	47.815	49.125	50.401	52.861
0.15	43.649	45.779	47.815	49.767	51.646	53.458	55.211	56.911	58.561	60.165	61.728	64.741
0.20	50.401	52.861	55.211	57.466	59.635	61.728	63.753	65.715	67.620	69.473	71.278	74.757
0.25	56.350	59.100	61.728	64.249	66.674	69.014	71.278	73.471	75.601	77.673	79.691	83.581
0.30	61.728	64.741	67.620	70.381	73.038	75.601	78.081	80.484	82.817	85.087	87.297	91.558
0.35	66.674	69.929	73.038	76.020	78.890	81.659	84.337	86.933	89.453	91.904	94.292	98.894
0.40	71.278	74.757	78.081	81.269	84.337	87.297	90.160	92.935	95.629	98.250	100.802	105.722
0.45	75.601	79.291	82.817	86.199	89.453	92.592	95.629	98.572	101.430	104.209	106.917	112.135
0.50	79.691	83.581	87.297	90.862	94.292	97.601	100.802	103.904	106.917	109.846	112.700	118.201
0.55	83.581	87.660	91.558	95.296	98.894	102.365	105.722	108.976	112.135	115.208	118.201	123.970
0.60	87.297	91.558	95.629	99.534	103.291	106.917	110.423	113.821	117.121	120.331	123.457	129.482
0.65	90.862	95.296	99.534	103.598	107.509	111.282	114.932	118.469	121.904	125.244	128.498	134.770
0.70	94.292	98.894	103.291	107.509	111.567	115.483	119.270	122.941	126.505	129.972	133.348	139.857
0.75	97.601	102.365	106.917	111.282	115.483	119.536	123.457	127.256	130.946	134.534	138.029	144.766
0.80	100.802	105.722	110.423	114.932	119.270	123.457	127.505	131.430	135.240	138.946	142.555	149.513
0.85	103.904	108.976	113.821	118.469	122.941	127.256	131.430	135.475	139.402	143.222	146.943	154.115
0.90	106.917	112.135	117.121	121.904	126.505	130.946	135.240	139.402	143.444	147.374	151.203	158.583
0.95	109.846	115.208	120.331	125.244	129.972	134.534	138.946	143.222	147.374	151.413	155.346	162.928
1.00	112.700	118.201	123.457	128.498	133.348	138.029	142.555	146.943	151.203	155.346	159.382	167.161
1.05	115.483	121.120	126.505	131.671	136.641	141.437	146.076	150.572	154.937	159.183	163.318	171.289
1.10	118.201	123.970	129.482	134.770	139.857	144.766	149.513	154.115	158.583	162.928	167.161	175.320
1.15	120.857	126.756	132.393	137.799	143.000	148.019	152.874	157.579	162.147	166.590	170.918	179.260
1.20	123.457	129.482	135.240	140.762	146.076	151.203	156.162	160.968	165.634	170.173	174.594	183.116
1.25	126.002	132.152	138.029	143.665	149.088	154.321	159.382	164.287	169.050	173.682	178.194	186.892
1.30	128.498	134.770	140.762	146.510	152.041	157.377	162.538	167.541	172.398	177.122	181.723	190.593

Radius (meters)

Coefficient of Friction (f)	240	260	280	300	330	360	390	420	450	480	510	540
0.05	39.040	40.635	42.168	43.649	45.779	47.815	49.767	51.646	53.458	55.211	56.911	58.561
0.10	55.211	57.466	59.635	61.728	64.741	67.620	70.38	73.038	75.601	78.081	80.484	82.817
0.15	67.620	70.381	73.038	75.601	79.291	82.817	86.199	89.453	92.592	95.629	98.572	101.430
0.20	78.081	81.269	84.337	87.297	91.558	95.629	99.534	103.291	106.917	110.423	113.821	117.121
0.25	87.297	90.862	94.292	97.601	102.365	106.917	111.282	115.483	119.536	123.457	127.256	130.946
0.30	95.629	99.534	103.291	106.917	112.135	117.121	121.904	126.505	130.946	135.240	139.402	143.444
0.35	103.291	107.509	111.567	115.483	121.120	126.505	131.67	136.641	141.437	146.076	150.572	154.937
0.40	110.423	114.932	119.270	123.457	129.482	135.240	140.762	146.076	151.203	156.162	160.968	165.634
0.45	117.121	121.904	126.505	130.946	137.337	143.444	149.30	154.937	160.375	165.634	170.732	175.682
0.50	123.457	128.498	133.348	138.029	144.766	151.203	157.377	163.318	169.050	174.594	179.967	185.185
0.55	129.482	134.770	139.857	144.766	151.832	158.583	165.058	171.289	177.301	183.116	188.751	194.224
0.60	135.240	140.762	146.076	151.203	158.583	165.634	172.398	178.906	185.185	191.258	197.144	202.860
0.65	140.762	146.510	152.041	157.377	165.058	172.398	179.437	186.211	192.747	199.068	205.194	211.143
0.70	146.076	152.041	157.780	163.318	171.289	178.906	186.211	193.240	200.023	206.583	212.940	219.114
0.75	151.203	157.377	163.318	169.050	177.301	185.185	192.747	200.023	207.043	213.833	220.414	226.804
0.80	156.162	162.538	168.674	174.594	183.116	191.258	199.068	206.583	213.833	220.846	227.643	234.243
0.85	160.968	167.541	173.865	179.967	188.751	197.144	205.194	212.940	220.414	227.643	234.649	241.452
0.90	165.634	172.398	178.906	185.185	194.224	202.860	211.143	219.114	226.804	234.243	241.452	248.452
0.95	170.173	177.122	183.808	190.259	199.546	208.419	216.929	225.118	233.019	240.661	248.068	255.260
1.00	174.594	181.723	188.583	195.202	204.730	213.833	222.563	230.966	239.073	246.913	254.512	261.891
1.05	178.906	186.211	193.240	200.023	209.786	219.114	228.061	236.670	244.977	253.011	260.798	268.359
1.10	183.116	190.593	197.788	204.730	214.722	224.270	233.428	242.239	250.742	258.965	266.935	274.674
1.15	187.231	194.877	202.233	209.331	219.548	229.311	238.674	247.684	256.377	264.785	272.934	280.847
1.20	191.258	199.068	206.583	213.833	224.270	234.243	243.807	253.011	261.891	270.480	278.804	286.887
1.25	195.202	203.173	210.842	218.243	228.895	239.073	248.835	258.228	267.292	276.057	284.554	292.803
1.30	199.068	207.196	215.018	222.565	233.428	243.807	253.763	263.342	272.585	281.524	290.189	298.602

Appendix E (Continued)
SPEED FROM SLIDESLIP OR YAW MARKS IN KILOMETERS PER HOUR

Radius (meters)

Coefficient of Friction (f)	570	600	650	700	750	800	850	900	950	1000
0.05	60.165	61.728	64.249	66.674	69.014	71.278	73.471	75.601	77.673	79.691
0.10	85.087	87.297	90.862	94.292	97.601	100.802	103.904	106.917	109.846	112.700
0.15	104.209	106.917	111.282	115.483	119.536	123.457	127.256	130.946	134.534	138.029
0.20	120.331	123.457	128.498	133.348	138.029	142.555	146.943	151.203	155.346	159.382
0.25	134.534	138.029	143.665	149.088	154.321	159.382	164.287	169.050	173.682	178.194
0.30	147.374	151.203	157.377	163.318	169.050	174.594	179.967	185.185	190.259	195.202
0.35	159.183	163.318	169.987	176.403	182.595	188.583	194.387	200.023	205.504	210.842
0.40	170.173	174.594	181.723	188.583	195.202	201.604	207.809	213.833	219.693	225.400
0.45	180.496	185.185	192.747	200.023	207.043	213.833	220.414	226.804	233.019	239.073
0.50	190.259	195.202	203.173	210.842	218.243	225.400	232.337	239.073	245.624	252.005
0.55	199.546	204.730	213.089	221.133	228.895	236.402	243.677	250.742	257.613	264.305
0.60	208.419	213.833	222.565	230.966	239.073	246.913	254.512	261.891	269.068	276.057
0.65	216.929	222.565	231.653	240.397	248.835	256.996	264.905	272.585	280.054	287.330
0.70	225.118	230.966	240.397	249.472	258.228	266.697	274.905	282.875	290.626	298.176
0.75	233.019	239.073	248.835	258.228	267.292	276.057	284.554	292.803	300.827	308.642
0.80	240.661	246.913	256.996	266.697	276.057	285.111	293.886	302.406	310.692	318.764
0.85	248.068	254.512	264.905	274.905	284.554	293.886	302.930	311.713	320.254	328.574
0.90	255.260	261.891	272.585	282.875	292.803	302.406	311.713	320.750	329.539	338.100
0.95	262.255	269.068	280.054	290.626	300.827	310.692	320.254	329.539	338.569	347.365
1.00	269.068	276.057	287.330	298.176	308.642	318.764	328.574	338.100	347.365	356.389
1.05	275.712	282.875	294.425	305.540	316.264	326.636	336.688	346.449	355.943	365.190
1.10	282.200	289.532	301.354	312.730	323.706	334.322	344.611	354.602	364.319	373.784
1.15	288.543	296.039	308.127	319.758	330.981	341.836	352.357	362.572	372.507	382.184
1.20	294.749	302.406	314.754	326.636	338.100	349.188	359.935	370.370	380.519	390.404
1.25	300.827	308.642	321.244	333.371	345.072	356.389	367.357	378.007	388.366	398.455
1.30	306.784	314.754	327.606	339.973	351.906	363.447	374.632	385.493	396.057	406.346

Appendix F

SQUARES AND SQUARE ROOTS*

*Reproduced with permission of Gage Educational Publishing Limited, Agincourt, Ontario, Canada.

Squares and Square Roots

n	n^2	$\sqrt{n}$	n	n^2	$\sqrt{n}$	n	n^2	$\sqrt{n}$	n	n^2	$\sqrt{n}$
1	1	1.000	51	2601	7.141	101	10,201	10.050	151	22,801	12.288
2	4	1.414	52	2704	7.211	102	10,404	10.100	152	23,104	12.329
3	9	1.732	53	2809	7.280	103	10,609	10.149	153	23,409	12.369
4	16	2.000	54	2916	7.348	104	10,816	10.198	154	23,716	12.410
5	25	2.236	55	3025	7.416	105	11,025	10.247	155	24,025	12.450
6	36	2.449	56	3136	7.483	106	11,236	10.296	156	24,336	12.490
7	49	2.646	57	3249	7.550	107	11,449	10.344	157	24,649	12.530
8	64	2.828	58	3364	7.616	108	11,664	10.392	158	24,964	12.570
9	81	3.000	59	3481	7.681	109	11,881	10.440	159	25,281	12.610
10	100	3.162	60	3600	7.746	110	12,100	10.488	160	25,600	12.649
11	121	3.317	61	3721	7.810	111	12,321	10.536	161	25,921	12.689
12	144	3.464	62	3844	7.874	112	12,544	10.583	162	26,244	12.728
13	169	3.606	63	3969	7.937	113	12,769	10.630	163	26,569	12.767
14	196	3.742	64	4096	8.000	114	12,996	10.677	164	26,896	12.806
15	225	3.873	65	4225	8.062	115	13,225	10.724	165	27,225	12.845
16	256	4.000	66	4356	8.124	116	13,456	10.770	166	27,556	12.884
17	289	4.123	67	4489	8.185	117	13,689	10.817	167	27,889	12.923
18	324	4.243	68	4624	8.246	118	13,924	10.863	168	28,224	12.961
19	361	4.359	69	4761	8.307	119	14,161	10.909	169	28,561	13.000
20	400	4.472	70	4900	8.367	120	14,400	10.954	170	28,900	13.038
21	441	4.583	71	5041	8.426	121	14,641	11.000	171	29,241	13.077
22	484	4.690	72	5184	8.485	122	14,884	11.045	172	29,584	13.115
23	529	4.796	73	5329	8.544	123	15,129	11.091	173	29,929	13.153
24	576	4.899	74	5476	8.602	124	15,376	11.136	174	30,276	13.191
25	625	5.000	75	5625	8.660	125	15,625	11.180	175	30,625	13.229
26	676	5.099	76	5776	8.718	126	15,876	11.225	176	30,976	13.267
27	729	5.196	77	5929	8.775	127	16,129	11.269	177	31,329	13.304
28	784	5.292	78	6084	8.832	128	16,384	11.314	178	31,684	13.342
29	841	5.385	79	6241	8.888	129	16,641	11.358	179	32,041	13.379
30	900	5.477	80	6400	8.944	130	16,900	11.402	180	32,400	13.416
31	961	5.568	81	6561	9.000	131	17,161	11.446	181	32,761	13.454
32	1024	5.657	82	6724	9.055	132	17,424	11.489	182	33,124	13.491
33	1089	5.745	83	6889	9.110	133	17,689	11.533	183	33,489	13.528
34	1156	5.831	84	7056	9.165	134	17,956	11.576	184	33,856	13.565
35	1225	5.916	85	7225	9.220	135	18,225	11.619	185	34,225	13.601
36	1296	6.000	86	7396	9.274	136	18,496	11.662	186	34,596	13.638
37	1369	6.083	87	7569	9.327	137	18,769	11.705	187	34,969	13.675
38	1444	6.164	88	7744	9.381	138	19,044	11.747	188	35,344	13.711
39	1521	6.245	89	7921	9.434	139	19,321	11.790	189	35,721	13.748
40	1600	6.325	90	8100	9.487	140	19,600	11.832	190	36,100	13.784
41	1681	6.403	91	8281	9.539	141	19,881	11.874	191	36,481	13.820
42	1764	6.481	92	8464	9.592	142	20,164	11.916	192	36,864	13.856
43	1849	6.557	93	8649	9.644	143	20,449	11.958	193	37,249	13.892
44	1936	6.633	94	8836	9.695	144	20,736	12.000	194	37,636	13.928
45	2025	6.708	95	9025	9.747	145	21,025	12.042	195	38,025	13.964
46	2116	6.782	96	9216	9.798	146	21,316	12.083	196	38,416	14.000
47	2209	6.856	97	9409	9.849	147	21,609	12.124	197	38,809	14.036
48	2304	6.928	98	9604	9.899	148	21,904	12.166	198	39,204	14.071
49	2401	7.000	99	9801	9.950	149	22,201	12.207	199	39,601	14.107
50	2500	7.071	100	10,000	10.000	150	22,500	12.247	200	40,000	14.142

BIBLIOGRAPHY

American Automobile Association: *Manual on Pedestrian Safety*. American Automobile Association, Washington, D.C., 1964.

American Motors (Canada) Limited: *1979 Technical Service Manual AMC* (A791001). American Motors (Canada) Limited, Brampton, Ontario, Canada, 1979.

Baker, J. Stannard: *Traffic Accident Investigation Manual*. Traffic Institute, Northwestern University, Evanston, Illinois, 1975.

British Columbia: *The British Columbia Air Brake Manual* (J00203). Motor Vehicle Branch, Province of British Columbia, Canada. (Undated).

British Columbia Research: *Motor Vehicle Accident Investigation Reports* (Various). British Columbia Research, Vancouver, Canada.

Canadian Association of Technical Accident Investigators and Reconstructionists: *Field Test Papers (various)*, Canada, 1987–1994.

Canada Safety Council: *Effectiveness of Studded Tires*. Canada Safety Council, Ottawa, Ontario, Canada, 1970.

Canadian Institute of Science and Technology: *Technical Mathematics and Traffic Engineering Reports* (Various). Canadian Institute of Science and Technology, Toronto, Canada.

Canadian Standards Association: *Canadian Metric Practice Guide* (CAN3-Z234.1-76). Canadian Standards Association, Ottawa, Canada, 1976.

Collins, J.C. and Morris, J.L.: *Highway Collision Analysis*. Charles C Thomas, Publisher, Springfield, Illinois, 1974.

Evans, Henry K.: *Traffic Engineering Handbook*. Institute of Traffic Engineers, New Haven, Connecticut, 1950.

Goldenson, R.M.: *The Encyclopedia of Human Behaviour*. Doubleday & Co., Inc., New York, 1970.

Institute of Traffic Engineers: *Transportation and Traffic Engineering Handbook*. Prentice-Hall, Inc., Englewood Cliffs, New Jersey, 1976.

Krech, D., Crutchfield, R.S. and Livson, N.: *Elements of Psychology*. Alfred A. Knopf, Inc., Publisher, New York, 1969.

National Safety Council: *Manual on Classification of Motor Vehicle Traffic Accidents*, 3rd ed. (ANSI D16.1). National Safety Council, Chicago, 1970.

National Safety Council: *Accident Facts* (Stock No. 021.57). National Safety Council, Chicago, 1977.

National Transportation Safety Board: *Highway Accident Reports* (Various). National Transportation Safety Board, Washington, D.C.

Navin, F.P.D.: *Accident Reconstruction Test Papers (Various)*. University of British Columbia, Vancouver, Canada, 1987–1994.

Rivers, R.W.: *On-Scene Traffic Accident Investigation Manual (Training Notes)*. Institute of Police Technology and Management, University of North Florida, Jacksonville, Florida, 1994.

Rivers, R.W.: *Speed Analysis for Traffic Accident Investigation Manual (Training Notes)*. Institute of Police Technology and Management, University of North Florida, Jacksonville, Florida, 1994.

Rivers, R.W.: *Traffic Accident Investigators' Handbook*. Charles C Thomas, Publisher, Springfield, Illinois, 1979.

Ruller, R.J.: *Accident Reconstruction Test Papers (Various)*. Queensland Police Service and Queensland University of Technology, Queensland, Australia, 1993–1994.

Schimizzi, Ned V.: *Mastering the Metric System*. New American Library, New York, 1975.

INDEX

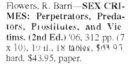
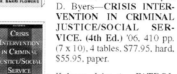
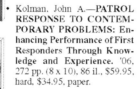

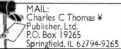